SLEEP
IS FOR THE
WEAK

EMILY-JANE CLARK

Emily-Jane Clark is a freelance journalist who lives in the East Midlands with two VERY lively daughters and one tired husband. She writes regularly for *Metro UK*, *Huffington Post*, *Good Housekeeping* online and the *New Statesman*. Other writing credits include *Mirror* online, *Femail*, *Kidspot*, *Scary Mommy* and the *Telegraph* online. She has written sketches for *Crooked Pieces* and Director's Cut Theatre and BBC Radio 4's *The Show What You Wrote* and was a finalist in the Funny Women Awards 2016. Emily-Jane is also a volunteer at Home-Start, a charity that helps families in need.

TO ISLA AND CLEO,
MY WONDERFULLY EXHAUSTING
LITTLE SLEEP THIEVES.

First published in Great Britain in 2017 by
Kyle Books, an imprint of Kyle Cathie Ltd
192-198 Vauxhall Bridge Road
London SW1V 1DX
general.enquiries@kylebooks.com
www.kylebooks.co.uk

10 9 8 7 6 5 4 3 2 1

ISBN 978 0 85783 431 7

Designer: Nicky Collings
Illustrator: Lorna Cowley
Project Editor: Sophie Allen
Editorial Assistants: Hannah Coughlin and
Isabel Gonzalez-Prendergast
Production: Nic Jones, Gemma John and
Lisa Pinnell

A Cataloguing in Publication record for this title is
available from the British Library.

Colour reproduction by ALTA, London
Printed in Slovenia by DZS Grafik d.o.o

Emily-Jane Clark

Illustrations by Lorna Cowley

Kyle Books

CONTENTS

A LITTLE WARNING ABOUT THE CONTENT OF THIS BOOK...

THIS BOOK CONTAINS SATIRE, SARCASM AND A BIT OF SWEARING

Thanks to the People Who Get All Offended By Silly Stuff I have to point out that this book is based on MY experience of babies. If you read this and think, 'Oh I don't do that with my babies – is this woman insinuating I am doing babies all wrong?' then you are one of these people. Just because I say I get my baby to sleep one way – does not mean that I believe that all the other ways are wrong. What I am trying to say is that if babies were cats and we lived in a world where homemade cat-skin jackets were all the rage (bear with me) and we all skinned our cats differently we would still ALL end up with beautiful cat-skin jackets. *

I also have to point out that not all babies are Sleep Thieves. I can confirm that other babies are available including Happy To Go Down Drowsy But Awake Baby, the Couple Of Times a Night Baby and even the rare Magical Sleep Through The Night Angel-Baby.

*By the way People Who Get All Offended By Silly Stuff, I am not endorsing the making of homemade cat-skin jackets.

INTRODUCTION: CAN YOU DIE OF SLEEP-DEPRIVATION?

Sleep-deprivation can kill. I know this because the Internet told me. It was about 4am and I was up yet again with my new baby. I needed answers. I needed to know that I would survive the torture of being kept awake, night after night, after night. So with my heart in my mouth, I frantically Googled, 'Can you die of sleep-deprivation?'

I was so shocked by what I found out that I woke up my husband, James, to break the news:

'James, James, wake up!' I cried, until he finally opened his eyes. 'I am going to die.'

I waved my mobile phone at him. 'It says here that in the 1980s this scientist bloke conducted a series of ground-breaking sleep experiments and, after staying awake for 32 days, all of his subjects died.' I should mention at this point in the story that those 'subjects' were rats. But still, it was a terrifying thing to discover after many months of barely any sleep.

'Well, in that case, you really ought to sleep while the baby sleeps instead of messing around on your phone,' groaned James, before rolling back over and (annoyingly) going straight back to sleep.

'Yes, sleep while you can my love,' I whispered manically into the darkness. 'Because soon I'll be dead and you'll have to deal with the baby every single night. Alone. See how you like that!'

So it is a fact. Sleep-deprivation can kill you, if you are a rat. But thankfully, if you are a human parent it probably won't.

I know this because I was severely sleep-deprived for four years and I did not die. I was exhausted, depressed, anxious and often felt like I was dying, but I lived to tell the tale. This tale.

I should start by telling you about my two daughters, aka the Sleep Thieves. The two tiny, beautiful girls who stole my heart, my sleep and almost my sanity.

 Babies wake up at night. I knew this going into motherhood. But my offspring didn't just wake up a few times for a feed or a nappy change. On a bad night, they woke up every half hour; on a good night, every few hours; and on a really bad night, they would just refuse to go to sleep at all. Born just 18 months apart, they were both highly adept in the art of wakefulness.

People told me things would improve.

'Babies settle down at six months,' they said.

'They will sleep better when they start on solids,' they reassured me.

'When they start crawling/walking/talking, they'll definitely sleep,' they promised.

'They' were liars. Mine did not. Both my children saw sleep as unnecessary until they were well into toddlerhood. As a result, I spent the first few years of motherhood living like some kind of weird zombie, surviving on reheated coffee and half-eaten biscuits.

Parenthood was nothing like I expected when I was expecting. I *expected* babies to be tucked up in bed by 8pm (because they're babies and they do as we say, right?). I envisaged my husband and me heading downstairs after we had kissed our little angel good night. Then we'd open a bottle of wine and happily bask in our post-baby bubble. I did not expect my daughter to wake up every half hour and scream the moment I put her back in her cot. Neither did I think that we would spend our evenings tensely watching TV with the subtitles on, not daring to talk, laugh or flush the toilet for fear we would 'wake the baby'. I expected to love my baby, but I didn't expect to fall in love with her and for it to give me strength I never knew I had. And I certainly did not expect to lose my first year of motherhood to postnatal depression and anxiety. In hindsight, the only thing I should have expected when I was expecting – was a baby.

I know what you are thinking, 'Why the hell are you writing a book when you could be sleeping, you dickhead?' Well, back when I was in the pits of sleep-deprivation, knowing that there were other babies who hated to sleep as much as (or more than!) mine always made me feel better. There was great comfort in knowing my child was not an alien freak baby and that I was not alone in my nightly battles. I also discovered that when it comes to parenting on barely any sleep, if you didn't laugh you would cry. A lot. And possibly never stop. So I guess I wrote this book in the hope it would provide some laughter and comfort to tired parents.

I can't tell you how to get your baby to sleep. I won't tell you how to get your baby to sleep. In fact, I have no sleep advice whatsoever. However, I can tell you that with the help of coffee, wine and a sense of humour – you will survive those sleepless nights.

> 'Through humour, we see in what seems rational, the irrational;
> in what seems important, the unimportant. It also heightens our sense
> of survival and preserves our sanity.'
>
> **Charlie Chaplin**

QUIZ: JUST HOW SLEEP-DEPRIVED ARE YOU?

If you are reading this book, then there is a good chance that you are suffering from sleep-deprivation. But just how tired are you? Are you bordering on brain dead? Drowsy but awake? Or meandering into madness? Find out by taking this totally pointless quiz:

Simply answer yes or no to the following questions:

1. Do you find it impossible to leave the house after 8pm?

2. Do you find it impossible to leave the house before 8am?

3. Do you sometimes watch the blue 'no signal' screen on TV because you are too tired to find the remote control?

4. Do you always fall asleep whenever you try to read a book that promises to tell you how to get your baby to fall asleep?

5. Have you ever cried because you have run out of coffee?

6. Do you take more than two hours to leave the house?

7. Do you have no idea where all the fucking socks go?

8. Are you too tired to stand up in the shower?

9. Do you have more than two piles of laundry?

10. Do you get angry at anything that makes a noise when your baby is asleep – the dishwasher beeping, the phone ringing or some twat ringing the doorbell?

11. Do you feel like 'tired' is your new personality?

12. Do you fantasise about having an operation, just so that you can get put to sleep?

13. Do you consider three hours' sleep to be a pretty decent night?

14. Do you mostly wear pyjamas?

15. Is 90% of your life spent silently creeping about in the dark?

16. Would you say that a morning triple-reheated coffee is the most important meal of the day?

17. Do you swear under your breath on a daily basis?

18. Is a trip to the dentist your idea of heaven?

19. Do you yell, 'Who the hell is ringing at this time?' at whatever time the phone rings?

20. Are you unable to remember anyone's name?

21. Have you ever tried to unlock your front door with your car key fob?

22. When someone tells you their baby 'sleeps through the night', do you want to punch them in the face?

23. Do you struggle to make simple decisions?

24. Do you sometimes stand up and have no idea what you actually stood up for?

25. Do you dread situations where you have to talk to other grown-ups?

26. Have you ever spent more than three hours trying to get your baby to have a 15-minute nap?

27. Do you occasionally cry over spilt milk?

28. Have you forgotten what it feels like to go to bed, and stay there, for an entire night?

29. Is it fairly normal for you to have been awake since 7am yesterday?

30. Do you claim your baby is sick to get out of social events?

31. Do you give your baby the finger behind her back?

32. Do you ever watch your partner sleeping and feel an urge to head butt them in the nose?

33. Have you ever squirted your own breast milk into your coffee because you have run out of milk?

34. Have you ever drunk alcohol before breastfeeding to see if it would help get the baby to sleep?

35. Do you feel really quite pleased when friends with 'good sleepers' tell you their baby is teething?

HOW DID YOU SCORE?

How many times did you answer **YES?**

20–40: TOTAL ZOMBIE SHIT BRAIN

I suspect you already know that you are extremely sleep-deprived. But do you realise you are also kicking arse? Taking care of a baby on no sleep is tough, yet you are doing it every single day!

TOP TIP

Why are you wasting time doing quizzes?
Go and have a nap now, before the baby wakes up.

10–20: DROWSY BUT AWAKE

You are exhausted, but caffeine and cake give you the power to get through the day.

TOP TIP

Make bedtime and dinner time more bearable
by switching from coffee to wine at 5pm.

0–10: JUST A BIT STUPID

Even if your baby does sleep, parenthood is tough. So it is inevitable that you will make silly mistakes from time to time.

TOP TIP

Just blame teething.
It's all teething's fault.

PART I

FROM BUMP TO BABY AND BEYOND (EXHAUSTED)

'100% OF BABIES DO NOT DO THINGS BY THE BOOK.'

THINGS I ACHIEVED IN THE FIRST THREE MONTHS OF MOTHERHOOD

1. I stuck two fingers up at the baby.
2. I answered the door with a breast out.
3. I literally cried over spilt milk.
4. I breastfed while on the loo.

WHAT TO EXPECT WHEN NOTHING IS ANYTHING LIKE YOU EXPECTED WHEN YOU WERE EXPECTING

'How are you finding motherhood?' people would ask me shortly after the arrival of my first baby.

'Great,' I would lie, fighting back the tears. 'It is the best thing ever.'

The truth is, I felt like crap. While all the other mums were hanging out at baby sensory groups, wearing clean clothes and preparing casseroles for dinner (probably), I was mostly sat in my pyjamas and crying. I felt that maybe I just wasn't cut out for motherhood. In hindsight, maybe I hadn't really thought the whole baby thing through.

My husband, James, brought up the subject one very hungover Sunday morning:

'Urgghh, we should stop drinking and have babies or something,' he groaned.

'Yes! I could do with a detox,' I agreed – before throwing up in the bin. And so the deal was done. We dumped the condoms and started 'trying' for a baby... with absolutely no concept of what having a baby would actually entail. But I had plenty of time to bone up on childcare. I read all the books. I subscribed to Babycentre. And then...

'We are going to be actual grown-up parents,' I exclaimed, waving a urine-covered stick in front of my husband's face, 'To a cute little baby!'

We bought a bottle of sparkling wine to celebrate – after sensibly consulting Google as to whether I could have a drink while pregnant. I discovered a wide range of opinions from 'just one' to 'never', so in the end I went with the most reputable source I could find (okay, the one that said you can actually have a glass of wine).

From that day forward my husband and I talked about nothing but baby names, prams and pregnancy symptoms. We decorated the spare room and spent entire evenings discussing 'things we need to do before the baby arrives'. We took turns to Google everything from electric breast pumps and baby poo charts to 'What the Hell is a Gro-bag?'

Sunday lunches at the pub were replaced with strolling around Mothercare hand-in-hand, smiling at babies and debating the pros and cons of three-wheeler buggies. We spoke of parenthood and how amazing it would be. We smiled, we laughed, we lay in each other's arms watching back-to-back episodes of *One Born Every Minute*.

It was a special time.

However, once the baby arrived the honeymoon was well and truly over.

'Where are the bloody colic drops?' I shouted into the darkness about ten nights into parenthood. 'I thought we agreed to keep some up here and some downstairs.'

No one answered me.

'James!' I screamed while trying to keep the crying baby from latching on to my nipple before I had administered the life-changing drops. 'Quick!' Five minutes later, James finally appeared with the colic drops. 'Well, it's too late. She's feeding now.'

'Oh for god's sake,' James replied, handing me the drops. 'I thought we'd agreed to leave one up here and one downstairs.'

'Piss off.'

And that was just week two. Our daughter wouldn't sleep, so we couldn't sleep. She cried for three hours every evening and we had **NO IDEA WHY.** We were sleep-deprived, stressed and really getting on each other's nerves. The love bubble we were cuddled up in pre-baby had burst and it soon became clear that despite reading all the books we were totally unprepared for the rollercoaster that is new parenthood.

However, the good thing about the Parenthood Rollercoaster is that the highs never stop coming but fortunately the lows get fewer and fewer and eventually you stop feeling like your life has been turned upside down. Then you WILL reach the point where you can honestly say that motherhood really is the best thing ever!

TOP TIP

Read your baby not the books.

2

HOW TO ACTUALLY PREPARE FOR YOUR FIRST BABY

Sleep, relax, watch films and go out for romantic dinners with your partner... Read all the parenting books... Subscribe to all the baby websites...

These are just some of the things parents-to-be do 'before baby arrives'. But I am here to tell you not to bother with any of them.

While you may be tempted to do this sort of stuff 'while you can', actually enjoying your last few child-free weeks should be avoided at all costs. It will only guarantee that the arrival of your baby will be an even bigger shock to your system!

Far better to ease yourselves into extreme tiredness, stress and chaos by taking the following steps:

1. Set your alarm to go off every hour between 8pm and 8am. On hearing the alarm, get up and wander around the house carrying a bag of flour. Shush and sing songs in the dark until you are about to pass out. Repeat every night.

2. During the day, continue to carry the bag of flour around the house. It is vital that you never put it down. You must eat, drink, tidy up and go to the toilet with the bag of flour cradled in your arm.

3. Do not sit down. Ever.

4. Consume only cold food and drink.

5. Never go to the toilet alone.

6. Get your senses accustomed to the new smells you are about to experience by spraying your sofa with fresh urine, vomit and milk.

7. Tie one arm behind your back and learn to perform all tasks with just one hand.

8. Buy one hundred baby socks, throw one of each pair in the bin and scatter the rest around the house.

9. Gather together everything you own that is nice and/or valuable. Cover it in snot and biscuit crumbs.

10. Forget having a shower every day. Learn to love your natural body odour (or at least get used to it).

11. Buy a second washing machine or save up for a cleaner. Because once you have a baby you will be doing laundry every day FOR THE REST OF YOUR LIFE.

12. Stock up on coffee.

13. Cover every surface with coloured plastic and dirty handprints.

14. Invest in a shed load of baby wipes.

15. Throw out all the baby 'expert' books. The only person who will be an 'expert' on your baby is you.

16. Ride on a rollercoaster with some balls. Juggle them while wiping a bum and continuously whispering, 'for fuck's sake'.

17. Throw up on all of your clothes. Leave the vomit to dry and then continue to wear your vomit-stained clothes for at least another 24 hours.

18. Never arrive anywhere on time.

19. Stop answering the phone and never reply to text messages.

20. Practise blaming everything on teething. Crying, grumpiness, lateness, missed appointments, tiredness, nappy rash or World War III. Once you have babies, everything is teething's fault.

21. While doing all of the above it is essential that you smile for a selfie and look suitably #blessed!

3

WHY THE HELL IS MY BABY NOT DOING THIS YET?

When I arrived home from hospital with my first baby, I became obsessed with everything being 'normal': Is what my baby doing normal? Am I normal? Is this normal? Is that normal?

I did everything I could to check that my newborn was progressing 'normally'. I studied developmental charts in the What To Expect books and signed up for those monthly newsletters that list all the things your little one really should be doing by now.

But the thing is, for every developmental 'milestone' my baby hit, there were at least five more that she hadn't hit. So, of course, I regularly panicked.

'Oh my god! My baby cannot roll over. She should be rolling over by now. What the hell is wrong with her?'

I would lay the baby on the floor and attempt to coax her into rolling. Nothing. I tried rolling about on the floor myself to show her how it's done. Nothing. I would give her a little shove... Nope. It was official. I had a non-rolling baby.

Unsurprisingly, she did roll eventually. But not before I'd called the health visitor, spoken to the doctor and spent many sleepless nights Googling, 'Why the hell isn't my baby rolling yet?'

So if you are a brand-new parent, a word of advice. Unsubscribe from all monthly 'milestone' emails and throw away the baby books. Go now, quickly, before the baby wakes up. Then come back and read this instead.

YOU AND YOUR NEW BABY (WHY MILESTONES ARE BOLLOCKS)

When it comes to babies, there is no such thing as 'normal'. Babies are strange little creatures who poo their pants, cry a lot and drink shit loads of milk. Yes, yes, okay, they are also really bloody cute but your bundle of joy has just spent the best part of a year floating around in a bubble. Chances are it's going to take her a bit of time to figure out how to do stuff.

Whatever your newborn looks like when she exits the womb, everyone will tell you she looks just like her father. Truth be told, new babies don't really look like anybody. They just look like new babies. Weird, blotchy babies, covered in crusty womb juice.

There's nothing 'normal' about being a parent to a very young baby. Pacing around the house in the night like a deranged zombie... discussing things like the texture of your child's poo... randomly bursting into tears for no apparent reason... There's nothing remotely 'normal' about carrying something around for 24 hours a day, right after you've had a human being removed from your body. Had any situation other than childbirth left you with stitches – **WHERE NO WOMAN SHOULD EVER HAVE STITCHES** – you would be lying in bed drinking chicken soup for at least three weeks.

From the moment you arrive home from the hospital, you'll progress from tears to tantrums and back again countless times. At some point you will enter a fog of sleep-deprived madness and believe you just cannot do this. There will be swearing, there will be screaming, but just as you are on the verge of a mental breakdown you'll hit the I Can Do Loads Of Shit With One Hand phase and then you'll realise that maybe you can do this after all. For about three days. Then you'll totally freak out as it dawns on you that you have to look after this tiny child forever. But rest assured, the What The Fuck Have I Done stage is typical among new parents, as is coming to terms with the reality that your new life is nothing like what you expected when you were expecting. But the good news is that this phase will soon be replaced by the next one, which is the awesome I Love My Baby So Much I Have Stared at Her For 45 Minutes (Because I am Too Tired To Move But Also Because She Is So Amazing) stage.

'DID I MENTION I HAVEN'T BATHED HER YET?'
#WOMBJUICE

Your baby may or may not sleep for longer than an hour at a time. She may barely sleep at all or snooze all day long. She may sleep through the night at six weeks or she may not sleep through the night for three years. She may like to sleep with you, on you, in a pram or in her own cot. All babies are different. But they do learn to sleep through the night eventually. And you will learn how to cope with not sleeping through the night eventually. But in the meantime, buy yourself some comfortable pyjamas and try not to worry.

As for sitting up, rolling over, walking, talking, waving and drinking from a cup… Your baby will almost certainly do all of these things at some point. **SO CHILL THE HELL OUT.**

Oh, and by the way, life will never be 'normal' again, but it will also never be boring!

TOP TIP

How to be a good parent in 3 easy steps:
1. Get up.
2. Drink coffee.
3. Don't break the baby.

HOW TO GET YOUR BABY TO GO TO SLEEP AND STAY ASLEEP WHEN SHE DOESN'T WANT TO SLEEP

You have had a baby. Congratulations! All those months of heartburn, Braxton Hicks, piles, backache and peeing your pants are finally over. The stress of childbirth is behind you. However, just so you know, that was the easy bit.

Before I actually became a mum, I assumed young babies only woke up two or three times a night for a feed or a nappy change and parenting during the night would go something like this:

1. The baby wakes up.
2. You feed/change the baby.
3. You put the baby back in the cot.
4. You both go back to sleep.
5. Repeat two or possibly three times, tops.

It turns out night time parenting is nowhere near that simple. This is what actually happened on a typical night for me:

ONE NIGHT IN THE LIFE OF A SLEEP–DEPRIVED MOTHER

It is 4am and I am in bed. Awake. Again. My baby has woken up at regular intervals since I put her to bed at 7.30pm. So by 4am I am seriously pissed off.

'For god's sake, what is her problem now?' I whisper angrily as I head to my daughter's cot once again.

I pick her up and she immediately stops crying. I sway her from side to side, but no lullaby. She is not getting a bloody lullaby at 4am.

I can feel her eyes looking up at me. 'Do not make eye contact,' I tell myself. 'Do not speak to her. Do not engage with her in any way. Any interaction will only encourage her to stay awake all night.'

She blows raspberries. I do not blink. She grabs my hair. I do not move. She gurgles something and quite deliberately makes it sound a bit like Mummy. I show no sign of weakness.

Her eyelids start to close and she looks drowsy. But I do not put her down. Not yet. The voices in my head make me falter; the Book Voices that come out at night to taunt me: 'Put her down drowsy but awake... do it now or she'll never sleep alone.' I ignore them. I have learnt that unless my daughter is practically in a coma before I place her in her cot, she will simply stay awake, and stay pissed off, for the entire night.

Finally her eyes close, her breathing becomes slow and heavy, and her 'limbs go limp'. So, according to Dr Sears, it is time. I creep over to the cot and prepare for the nerve-wracking transfer. I hold my breath and slowly, slowly lower her over the bars.

So far, so good. I lay her down, keeping my arm underneath her for a few minutes… just to be sure. Still asleep. I carefully perform the terrifying Arm Release Roll manoeuvre. Still asleep. I put her blanket over her. Still asleep. I tiptoe back to my bed, slide under the covers and close my eyes. The pearly gates of dreamland are just within my reach.

And then… A torturous scream pierces the blissful silence of the night and snatches me from my slumber once again.

'Right, that is it!' I think to myself. 'I have had enough of this every night. I am not getting up again. No more Mrs Nice Mummy. I am going to stay right here and close my eyes.'

'WAHH.'

'Bring it on baby. I am done. I am going to sleep.' I put the pillow over my head in an attempt to block out the screams.

'WAAAHHHHH.'

The screams are louder now, but I don't care. I am staying in bed.

'WAAHHHHH. WAHHH.'

Ok, I am getting out of bed.

And I am back at Square One. Holding a baby in the darkness. Rocking, shushing and praying for the strength to make it through tomorrow after another sleepless night. As silent tears roll down my cheeks, I long for sleep. I want to be alone. I want it to be 'before' again. But I chose this. I wanted this life. I made my bed and now I am lying in it. Awake.

My daughter looks up at me and smiles. I kiss her little cheeks and feel bad for being so miserable. I should be cherishing this moment, shouldn't I?

For I cherish my daughter. I really, really do. But this moment, right now, where I have snot and tears pouring down my face, sick in my hair and I feel physically and emotionally drained? This moment can piss right off.

She is still awake so I play the white noise app on my phone. Music box, ocean waves, rainfall…

Still awake.

I ask her really nicely to go to sleep. I bribe her. I beg her.

Still awake.

I lie her down in the cot and activate the new lullaby machine in the vague hope that tonight *will* be the night she'll be soothed gently into a deep sleep. She immediately screams. I leave her for a minute – waiting for the (bloody five-star-rated) dream machine to do its work. It doesn't. She screams some more and I get her out.

She's now wide awake and in a very bad mood.

I lay her down in my bed next to me and feed her. I have been trying to wean her off the night feeds, but my method – If She Screams Really Loudly I Will Just Bloody Feed Her – doesn't appear to be working. Still, at least I can get on with some useful things like picking up my phone and Googling stuff that parents really shouldn't Google when they're sleep-deprived at 4am. 'Can you die/get some horrible disease from exhaustion?', 'Is my baby broken?', 'How much sleep do babies need to survive?'

She has finished feeding, but she is still awake.

I am so exhausted I can barely stand up, so I resort to desperate measures and go with the Sod It She Can Sleep In My Bed approach, more commonly known as co-sleeping. I lie down and pretend to be asleep as she pulls my hair, bites my nose and tries to climb on my head. (No mention of all of this in the Attachment Parenting books.) But finally, finally, finally…

She sleeps.

She looks beautiful in her slumber. And at 9pm, 10pm or even 11pm I might have gazed lovingly at her for a few minutes. *BUT NOT AT STUPID PAST 4AM!* I am so over it now. Desperately seeking sleep, I lie precariously on the edge of the bed. Despite her size she seems to take up most of the space. But I dare not move. One cough, sneeze or bed creak and I will be right back at Square One.

My body is tired but my mind is now wide awake, asking the same old questions again and again. 'Why does my baby not sleep? Everyone else's baby sleeps. Why am I so rubbish at babies? How will I manage to get up and look after the baby tomorrow? *WILL I BE ABLE TO COPE?'*

Then the shrill sound of the Book Voices returns to haunt me: 'Well… now you've done it. See that beautiful baby asleep in your bed? That is a big fat rod for your own back. She'll have to sleep with you for the rest of her life. She'll become one of those lonely spinster cat ladies and it will be all your fault!'

Eventually my aching muscles sink into the mattress and I doze off… for about an hour and a half. At which point, I am rudely awoken by my husband's alarm. And after whisper-shouting, 'Press that snooze button again and I will bloody kill you!' my day begins.

So I get up, get dressed (eventually) and get on with it. And as I play with my little girl, I think to myself that actually I am not that rubbish at babies. My house is a mess, I can't get my head around anything more complicated than the Tweenies, but my child is happy and healthy so for today at least, I am kicking sleep-deprivation's arse…

It is amazing how much better things look after a good… 90 minutes sleep…

So, how do you get your baby to go to sleep and stay asleep when she doesn't want to sleep?

By whatever means necessary.

Still awake? Then the only thing you can do is wait… and wait… and wait for it to pass.

THE A-Z OF SLEEP-DEPRIVED PARENTING:

A GLOSSARY OF USEFUL TERMS YOU WON'T FIND IN THE BABY BOOKS

A **Awake But Drowsy**: Putting a baby in the cot this way is the fastest way to piss off your baby.

B **Baby-trapped**: Term used to describe being stuck under a sleeping baby who will wake up if you even think about moving.

C **Co-No Sleeping**: A popular technique also known as Too Tired To Care About The Bloody Rod.

D **Dream Crasher**: A baby or young child who always wakes up at the exact moment their parent falls asleep.

E **Expert Baby Advice Books**: Useful for propping up one end of the baby's cot when she has a cold.

F **For Fuck's Sake**: Most commonly used phrase of a sleep-deprived parent.

G **Good Night's Sleep**: Four hours in bed.

H **Hitting The Wall**: The point at which a parent believes they are too tired to go on any more. Running away or jumping out of the window is often considered, but curling up on the bathroom floor and crying is usually opted for.

I **Insomnia**: Also known as Mumsomnia. The rare occasion when a baby sleeps through the night, but the mother cannot.

J **Just Go The Fuck To Sleep**: Second most commonly used phrase of a sleep-deprived parent.

K **Kicking Arse**: What sleep-deprived parents do every single day.

L **Loo**: A sanctuary for tired mums.

M **Mumtrum/Mantrum**: When a mother or father finally snaps. Common causes are bedtime, running out of coffee and dinner time.

N **No-Sleep Solutions**: Survival strategies for the exhausted parent. Include coffee, wine and grandparents.

O **Operation**: A general anesthetic is the ultimate fantasy of many tired parents.

P **Pyjamas**: The standard uniform of the sleep-deprived parent.

Q **Quiet Or I Will Stab You**: A rule that must be adhered to when entering the home of a sleeping baby.

R **Risk Assessment**: Once a baby is finally asleep, parents assess every action that could potentially wake the baby. Risks include flushing the toilet, opening the front door and 'having an early night' (wink wink).

S **Sleep Thief**: A baby who steals a parent's sleep every single night.

T Teething: Term used to describe a baby who is being a pain in the arse.

U Under a baby: The place a sleep-deprived parent spends most of their time.

V Vacant: The look in a tired parent's eyes when you talk to them about politics/*The X Factor* or what they are doing next week.

W Witching Hour: When kids turn into little shits for no apparent reason.

X Xhausted: When a parent is too tired to think of a word beginning with 'x'.

Y Yawning: How sleep-deprived parents communicate with each other.

Z Zen: The feeling a parent gets when a baby finally goes to sleep.

FUN FACT

Did you know that sleep-deprivation was used as a form of torture by the KGB and the Japanese during World War II?

Did you also know that many new parents are tortured in this way on a regular basis, yet they still manage to get up and take care of their babies.

New parents are well hard.

HOW MUCH SLEEP DOES MY BABY REALLY NEED?

According to the infant sleep guidelines by The Academy Of Experts Who Have No Idea How Human Babies Actually Work, *'Sleeping fewer than the recommended hours is associated with attention, behaviour and learning problems. Insufficient sleep also increases the risk of accidents, injuries, hypertension, obesity, diabetes and depression.'*

So basically, if your baby doesn't sleep she is fucked.

The 'recommended time' usually goes by the ridiculous notion that in a 24 hour day, four- to 12-month-olds should sleep 12–16 hours; one- to four-year-olds should sleep 11–14 hours and three- to five-year-olds should be packing away a whopping 10–13 hours of slumber!

While some babies may well sleep for this length of time, many just don't, won't and never will.

I struggle to see the point of these guidelines. After all, we do not deliberately prevent our little ones from sleeping. We don't wake them up every 30 minutes or spend four hours doing bedtime for fun! We are not idiots. Most parents would love their offspring to sleep for 16 hours a day. But the fact is, if they don't, there is nothing we can do about it. All human babies are different. Just like adults, some need more sleep than others. The only way these charts would be useful, is if they came with a recipe for a potion that enabled all babies to sleep for the 'correct' number of hours every night. But unfortunately, they do not. Thankfully, however, The Institute of Real Life People With Actual Babies has provided a far more accurate guide for new parents:

HOW MUCH SLEEP YOUR BABY SHOULD ACTUALLY BE HAVING

AGE	NAPS	NIGHT
0–1 MONTH	Enough to make you feel a little bit smug	0–12 hours
1–3 MONTHS	1- 3, but only in a moving car or on you	Not much due to all the damn feeding
3–6 MONTHS	Occasionally, but only on you (not so smug now, are you?)	For as long as it takes you to get into bed and close your eyes
6–12 MONTHS	Unlikely	Not very much. All the people who told you they would sleep when they were on solids are liars
1–2 YEARS	Whatever. Are they even a thing?	Who fucking cares?

THE REAL REASONS WHY YOUR BABY IS AWAKE

Human babies wake up during the night. This is a fact. Unfortunately, as they can only communicate with cries, screams or growls (or is that just my babies?), the tricky bit is working out why.

As we stagger towards our screaming bundles of joy for the fuckteenth time, we desperately try to figure out what is wrong with them. Are they teething? Hungry? Do they have wind? Or are they just messing with us? Thanks to new research by The Institute of Actual People With Real Life Babies, the reasons why babies wake up during the night have finally been uncovered. Here are some of them:

* Your baby's going through a phase or a growth spurt or a phase of spurting growth. Or possibly a growth that spurts phases. Whatever it is, it's keeping her awake.

* You put her down drowsy but awake.

* You didn't put her down drowsy but awake.

* It's sleep regression. This is good news because according to everyone else who has ever had a baby there is always a worse sleep regression to come. 'You think the four-month regression is bad? Oh, wait until you hit month five…' So take heart, because in a couple of months you'll be looking back at this phase longingly.

* Your baby's unwell (although she's magically cured the moment you take her out of her cot).

* She wants to sleep in your bed.

* She doesn't want to sleep in your bed. She just wants to prat about in your bed. All night.

* She's teething.

* She's not teething.

* She absolutely is teething.

* Nope. She's not teething.

* She's definitely, certainly teething this time. Isn't she?

* She's not teething. Where are her damn teeth?

* She has wind. (Or she fancies a backrub because it's been two hours since you fed her and still no burp…)

* She's bored. After all, it is not like she can go down the pub. Crying is all she's got.

* She wants to prevent you and your partner from making another baby.

* She is evil.

* You didn't sleep train her.

* You did sleep train her and now she's making you pay.

* You fed/rocked/sang/cuddled her to sleep.

* You didn't feed/rock/sing/cuddle her to sleep.

* She needs a cuddle. Outside the womb is scary as shit.

PART II

HOW TO GET YOUR BABY TO GO THE FUCK TO SLEEP

'99% OF BABIES BELIEVE THAT SELF-SOOTHING IS BOLLOCKS.'

THINGS I ACHIEVED IN THE FIRST SIX MONTHS OF MOTHERHOOD

1. I bought 15 books on how to get babies to sleep.

2. I downloaded 12 white noise apps.

3. I bought 18 baby sleep toys.

4. I maxed out the credit cards.

HOW TO SURVIVE THE 'EXPERT' SLEEP ADVICE

'Sixteen hours, they say she needs! What are we doing wrong?' I yell at James, who rolls over sleepily to join me for our nightly discussion. 'Is she hungry? Is she teething? Is she not tired? Is she too tired? Is she sick? Is she a bloody vampire?'

'Well, did you try to put her down drowsy but awake?' James enquired. 'Yes, Mr Gina Bloody Ford, I did. The only problem with that little idea is that she loses her shit as soon as I place her in the cot.'

I had been a mum for six months and still had no idea how to get my baby to go to sleep or stay asleep. I had read all the books. I knew all the 'stuff'. I had been aware of growth spurts, sleep regression and separation anxiety even before my baby had been born. I could prevent nappy rash and spot the signs of meningitis. But knowing all the 'stuff' had not made motherhood any easier.

My baby did not do things by the book. Especially when it came to sleep.

'Babies should sleep around ten hours per night and have three naps per day,' I had read. Not *my* daughter. She had laughed in the face of sleep since day one and, as a result, I was exhausted and stressed. I felt like a failure.

I *thought* I knew what my baby needed. But somewhere in between *What To Expect When You're Expecting*, Mumsnet and countless revolutionary sleep advice books, I had lost the ability to trust my gut feeling.

I *felt* my daughter needed to be close to me while she slept. My gut was telling me that she did not yet feel secure enough to sleep alone. She was tiny. She was just 5lb 10oz (2.5 kilos) when she was born and maybe she instinctively felt vulnerable when she was away from me. But what the hell did my gut know? My gut hadn't got any childcare qualifications. My gut hadn't written a book. My gut didn't have its own TV show or 68 million followers on Twitter.

I had read it was bad to co-sleep. It could put my baby at risk and I would be 'making a rod for my own back.' She would never learn to sleep alone. I read that I shouldn't feed my baby to sleep. Not unless I wanted her still sucking on my wrinkly granny tits at 40 years old. So I continued to battle her back into her cot every half hour to an hour. I tried not to feed her despite it being the quickest, calmest way to get her back to sleep.

My Common Sense screamed at me: 'Let her sleep with you. Feed her when she wants. And get some bloody sleep. Problem solved.'

'SHUT THE HELL UP, COMMON SENSE', I THOUGHT. I AM JUST A MUM.

I will not bugger up my child by ignoring the all-important 'expert' advice. So I did everything the 'right' way and ended up severely sleep-deprived, anxious and depressed. I ignored my maternal instincts and did things that felt wrong because I thought they were 'right'. And yet, my baby still wouldn't sleep.

As time passed, motherhood had taken its toll on my mental health, my marriage, my physical health and my self-esteem. So I read more advice books.

'A good night's sleep is essential to your baby's brain development. A baby needs to be taught how to be a good sleeper,' the 'experts' claimed. I had got to the point where I felt guilty for *not* leaving my baby to cry. What kind of mother cuddles her baby when she screams? Was I being cruel by not letting her cry herself to sleep?

So in desperation one night, my husband and I left our daughter to cry. We had tried all the gentle training methods and nothing had worked so this was our last hope. It was the worst ten minutes of my life. Yep, just ten minutes of my baby screaming for comfort was all it took for me to realise that I had been an idiot.

I brought her into my bed and held her in my arms. She was so upset it took most of the night to settle her back to sleep. As I looked at her little face drenched with tears and listened to her struggling to get her breath back after all her crying, I decided there and then to stop giving a fuck what the 'experts' said. From that day forward I would Mum The Hell Up and do what I felt was best for my baby.

TOP TIP

BEDTIME:
If at first you don't succeed...
give up and go and eat cake.

KEEPING A BABY SLEEP LOG

While most baby 'experts' encourage new parents to keep a sleep log – in order to determine just how much your baby sleeps – I certainly wouldn't bother. I found that having proof of how little my baby slept only served to freak me out. Here's one I did earlier:

MY BABY SLEEP LOG

TIME WOKE	WHAT YOU DID	TIME WENT BACK TO SLEEP
8 PM	Fed her to sleep.	8.30 PM
9.10 PM	Tried putting her down drowsy. She kicked off. Fed her.	10 PM
10.35 PM	Cuddled, rocked and sang to her.	11.30 PM
12.15 AM	Prayed.	1 AM
1.20 AM	Begged.	
1.45 AM	Cried.	
2 AM	Gave her to Daddy.	Whatever.
2.10 AM	She wanted Mummy. Retrieved her from Daddy. Daddy is a dick.	Fuck knows.
3 AM	Did some swearing.	Still awake.
4 AM	Put her in bed with me.	5 AM
6 AM	You have got to be kidding me!	GO THE FUCK TO SLEEP

SLEEP-TRAINING TECHNIQUES (FOR DUMMIES)

When it comes to getting babies to sleep, there is an abundance of advice available on the Internet, in books and from random strangers in the supermarket.

Whether you are looking to bed share with your baby, leave them to cry or have some fun with Ferberization, there really is a sleep-training method for everyone.

To help you decide how best to train your offspring, here is a comprehensive guide to some of the most popular techniques:

1) THE EXTINCTION METHOD (ALSO KNOWN AS CRY IT OUT)
It is common knowledge that if your baby is unable to 'self-soothe' within a few months, she will turn into an obese sociopath who will still need you to help her sleep for the rest of your life. Therefore, it is best to teach your child to be self-sufficient from day one. Simply kiss her goodnight, turn out the light and leave the room. As long as she is fed, dry and left a few snacks there is no reason why she cannot be left alone indefinitely.

2) CONTROLLED CRYING
This method is perfect for parents who prefer their babies to cry in manageable, bite-sized chunks. Instead of leaving your baby to scream continuously, pop into her room at regular intervals throughout the night to show her what she is missing. However, do not pick her up, touch her or even look at her. Simply tell her to, 'Go back to sleep' – ideally in the voice of Samuel L. Jackson – and then leave the room.

3) THE NO-CRY SLEEP SOLUTION
This method is great for the parent who wants to sleep train their baby and get fit at the same time. The idea is to spend the entire night picking

up, putting down, picking up, putting down, picking up, putting down, picking up and putting down your baby – until you pass out.

4) Gradual Retreat (Into Insanity)
A technique that puts the fun back into bedtime! Spend entire nights playing How Many Millimetres Will I Make It Away From The Cot Before The Baby Kicks Off Again?

5) Co-Sleeping /Bed sharing
Simply lie down next to your baby and pretend to be asleep while they poke you, pull your hair and climb on your head. After two to four hours they will fall into a deep slumber on top of you or across the entire bed. To ensure that they stay asleep for longer than 10 minutes, you must lie completely still. Breathing, sneezing, coughing or thinking about moving them into a cot should be avoided.

6) Reluctant Co-sleeping
Similar to co-sleeping, but for people who are serious about not letting their baby sleep in their bed, like, EVER... until 4am when they have been up all night and they no longer give a shit about making a rod for their own back.

7) Get Your Baby To Sleep By Whatever Means Necessary
This is a popular technique used by parents of babies who are particularly averse to sleep. Instead of adhering to one particular method, you do whatever the hell it takes (with the exception of drugs and alcohol) to get your baby to fall asleep. A drive in the car, a feed, watching TV or a midnight Jumperoo session are all good options.

8) WOMB IMITATORS

Research shows that 100 per cent of babies wake up at night because they are wondering, 'Where the fuck is my womb?' After spending most of their life inside a female human, sleeping alone in the real world can be scary as hell. Fortunately, there is a thriving baby sleep industry ready to 'help' tired parents with night wakings. For just a few pounds you can purchase a Womb Imitator in the form of a cuddly toy, special mattress, an app or a cot mobile – all of which promise to trick your little one into thinking she is still inside you. (Unfortunately human wombs are not yet available to purchase, but watch this space as if no-one buys this book I might need to sell mine.)

9) THE ONLY TOTALLY FAILPROOF BABY SLEEP METHOD IN THE WORLD

This method is designed for those babies who spit in the eye of all sleep training. With a 100 per cent success rate, the Wait For Them Not To Be Babies Any More technqiue uses a unique combination of common sense, instincts and a sense of humour.

WARNING!

Before undertaking sleep training, is it essential that parents take the necessary precaution: stock up on wine.

FUN FACT

Every time a parenting 'expert' says the secret to getting a baby to sleep is a 'consistent bedtime routine' a kitten DIES.

HOW TO TEACH YOUR BABY TO SLEEP THROUGH THE NIGHT (EVENTUALLY)

So you have done the research, bought the books and selected a sleep-training method that is right for your family. Now it is time to begin. Simply follow this week-by-week guide and success is guaranteed!

BEFORE YOU BEGIN

STEP 1 Spend the first six months of parenthood in your pyjamas trying to get your baby to sleep.

STEP 2 After discovering that everybody else's baby apparently sleeps through the night, set aside approximately one month to read 'expert' sleep advice books and search the Internet for sleep solutions.

STEP 3 Attend weekly appointments with your health visitor to find out what is actually wrong with your child.

STEP 4   Spend several weeks wandering about the house like a braindead blob of human flesh.

You are now ready to begin sleep training. Good luck!

THE METHOD

Make the decision that you must sleep train your baby tonight.

By night time, you are too exhausted to sleep train your baby. Postpone sleep training until the following day.

The next day you are still too tired.

Four days later you are slightly less tired. Decide to start sleep training right away.

Put baby into her cot drowsy but awake. (Baby will immediately scream her head off.)

Tell baby calmly, 'It is sleep time' and leave the room. (Baby will scream even louder.)

Immediately return to the baby's room and pick the baby up. (Wonder if baby might be teething.)

Tell partner the baby might possibly be teething. Both decide to postpone sleep training for a bit.

A few days later, decide to commence sleep training again.

This time it is your partner's turn to put the baby down. (Baby will start screaming immediately.) Partner should leave the room. (Baby will scream even louder.)

Discuss with partner how long you should leave baby for. Five minutes, maybe? (More screaming.)

Tell partner you are going in. (Partner will point out that it has only been 45 seconds.) Wait another minute. (Baby will scream some more.)

Discuss possibility that baby might have banged her head or been sick. Go and get the baby.

Both fuss over the baby and feel guilty for leaving her to cry for **THREE WHOLE MINUTES.**

Decide to research a different sleep-training method in the morning that does not involve crying.

The baby will stay awake all night to make it clear she was not happy about the sleep-training attempt.

The next day you are so tired you forget about the plan to sleep train the baby.

Two weeks later you pass out in the supermarket from exhaustion and vow to definitely sleep train the baby that evening.

Put baby in the cot. (Baby will scream immediately.)

Pick baby up, cuddle her, and then – just as she is looking comfortable in your arms – put her back in the cot. (Baby will start crying again.)

Pick baby up, cuddle her, put her down, pick her up, cuddle her, put her down.

Repeat the above step over and over again until you are too tired to stand up, then text partner, 'It is your turn to sleep train the baby.'

Partner continues with the pick up, cuddle, put down routine until his smart phone runs out of battery.

Take over the baby routine yourself until you are on the verge of a nervous breakdown.

Lay the baby in your bed for a 'few minutes' and fall asleep for the last hour of night time.

The next day decide you must find a sleep-training method that involves less effort.

A week later, decide you must sleep train your baby tonight. *WITHOUT FAIL.*

Put baby down in her cot. Do not leave the room. Instead 'gradually retreat' to a seat, next to the cot. (Baby will throw her dummy out of her cot and scream for her dummy.)

Give baby back her dummy, baby throws out dummy.

Repeat the dummy routine ten times.

The baby will continue to cry, but you must reassure her that she is perfectly okay because you are right next to her. (The baby won't seem reassured.)

Try singing baby a lullaby. (She probably won't hear it over the screaming.)

Compromise by stroking the baby's head. (The baby will now be even more upset because she thought you were going to pick her up, not stroke her head.)

Attempt to fob off the baby by giving her a sheep that makes womby noises. (Baby will throw the sheep on the floor.)

Attempt to cuddle baby through the bars. (Arm will get stuck, baby will hold on to stuck arm for dear life and bite arm.)

Wriggle arm free. (Baby will now be so angry she will bang her chin on the cot.)

Lift baby out for a cuddle and postpone sleep training until tomorrow due to chin injury and bitten arm.

The next day the baby seems a bit grumpy. Decide she might be coming down with something and delay sleep training just in case.

It's the baby's first birthday and you realise that you have barely slept in an entire year.

Make the decision that you absolutely must sleep train the baby.

That night, partner takes baby up to her room. Ten minutes later, partner returns downstairs.

Partner confesses he did not put her down drowsy but awake because, 'She fell asleep on me'.

Have a row with partner about the importance of putting the baby down 'drowsy but awake'.

Decide it is pointless continuing with sleep training tonight as partner has 'buggered it up'.

Both sulk for two days and then decide to definitely, definitely, start sleep training. No. Matter. What.

On the third night of very 'gradually retreating' nowhere, baby sleeps for five hours straight. You believe you have turned a corner.

Tell everyone you know the baby is practically sleeping through the night. Announce on Facebook the baby is practically sleeping through the night. The next night the baby wakes up twelve times.

One month later the only place you are gradually retreating into is madness and the baby is still waking up most of the night, every night. It dawns on you that you are actually more exhausted now than before you started sleep training.

You quit sleep training, stop Googling about sleep training, stop worrying about the baby not sleeping and finally accept that your baby is not sleeping. You resign yourself to the fact that the Sleep Thief has won. Then, and only then, will your baby sleep (probably).

12

IF YOU DON'T SLEEP TRAIN YOUR BABY WILL SHE BE AWAKE FOREVER?

Every baby is unique, every family situation is different and when it comes to sleeping – there is no 'one size fits all'. If you're considering sleep training your baby, and don't know where to start, here are a few helpful suggestions:

★ If you don't think your baby is ready for sleep training, don't do it.

★ If you are sleep training your baby because all the other mums at playgroup are doing it, don't do it. All babies are different.

★ If you are sleep training your baby because a book said you should – and you believe the writer knows better than you because they wrote an actual book (while you only have a degree in drama and English) – don't do it. You are the only 'expert' on your baby.

★ If you are sleep training your baby because you read a study that said it is the best thing for babies, don't do it.

* If you are training your baby because you are scared that her development might suffer if she does not sleep through the night, don't do it. Babies have been waking up in the night since babies were invented and the world isn't full of middle-aged sickly weirdoes who still haven't learnt to talk/walk/use a knife and fork.

* If you are sleep training your baby because it feels right for you and your family, then try it.

WARNING!

If you do decide to try sleep training, remind yourself that having a baby who wakes up a lot is tough. The half hourly wakings, 4am pyjama parties, entire nights without any sleep, no evenings to yourself, no time with your partner, the vomit in your hair, cold coffee, feeling sick with exhaustion, self-doubt, tears and anxiety all take their toll on you and stretch you to the limit.

You are taking care of a tiny baby while feeling like a zombie. If you try a sleep method and decide to give up after a few days, an hour or even five minutes then it is totally understandable. You have not failed. If you try one way, then another way and still she won't sleep, then you have not failed. If you try co-sleeping and your offspring still won't settle, you have not failed. It is just not the right way for your child.

Like adults, some babies sleep through the night, and some don't. But things will get better. One day you will be up, dressed and drinking a tepid coffee after only a few hours' sleep. You will smile at your happy, healthy baby and realise that she has successfully trained you NOT to sleep through the night.

HAVE YOU BEEN DOING B.E.D.T.I.M.E WRONG YOUR ENTIRE LIFE?

Do you hate bedtime? Does it consistently make you miserable? Do you routinely spend most of the night in a dark room with a baby? Have you been consistently routining your arse off since day one, and yet your baby still won't sleep? Then this seven step **B.E.D.T.I.M.E** routine is for you:

B   BEDTIME ROUTINE:

It is vitally important that you have a consistent bedtime routine that is routinely consistent at bedtime. For best results, consistently use a bed, a baby and a time.

E   EXPECTATIONS:

Lower them. A bit more. Lower... That's it. Now any sleep at all is a bonus.

D **DROWSY BUT AWAKE.**

Is your baby fast asleep in your arms? Then you have failed already. As soon as your baby is comfortable, content and on the verge of nodding off to dreamland, you must put her down immediately.

T **TIRED (BUT NOT TOO TIRED)**

Is your baby a little bit tired? Is she yawning, but just slightly? More importantly, are you in desperate need of a glass of wine before you totally lose your mind? Then stop whatever you are doing and begin *B.E.D.T.I.M.E* immediately.

I **INFORMATION:**

Under no circumstances should a bedtime routine be attempted until you have read all the information on all the Internets and in all the books in the entire world. Because (according to the 'experts'), parents are idiots who would never have even thought about trying a 'routine'.

M **MAGICAL SLEEP MAKERS:**

'This Magical Sleep Maker will help your baby settle into a peaceful slumber and therefore develop normally and not turn into an unhinged sociopath with obesity issues. If you love your baby, you will spend many pounds on this item right now.'

Parents are advised to invest in many Magical Sleep Makers, which are available in book, toy, app, music, gadget or consultation form. While purchasing these products may not actually get your baby to sleep, they do allow you to enjoy a small glimmer of hope while you wait to try them. Only once you have spent hundreds of pounds on Magical Sleep Makers, and lost all hope, will you be ready to embark on the final stage of the *B.E.D.T.I.M.E* routine.

E   ENVIRONMENT:

'A calm, quiet environment is the best place to help your child get to sleep,' say the book 'experts' (because remember, us parents are idiots). To create this environment, you need a quiet room, a cot and some calm...

BUT the only thing you and your partner have said to each other in months is 'it's your turn'. Your lives consist of trying to get your offspring to sleep and trying to get some sleep yourselves. You and your partner are like shipwrecks passing in the night, shadows of the people you once were. Your beautiful baby is tearing you apart.

You rock, shush, sing and feed a baby in a quiet room for hours and hours every evening. You are desperately lonely but never alone. You are constantly busy but nothing gets done. There is no time or space to think, talk, rest or breathe. The exhaustion is relentless and all-consuming. You are tired and miserable but at least you are **FUCKING CONSISTENT**. You are on the verge of a breakdown, but that is okay because you are sticking to the damn **ROUTINE**.

Considering all of this, there is a good chance your 'calm environment' is well and truly buggered. So it is time to try the unthinkable. To go where no Supernanny has ever gone before. Gina Ford may well have 'contented' kittens at the thought of this, but to hell with it...

Forget **B.ED.T.I.M.E.** Give consistency the finger and tell the routine to do one.

Take your baby into another room, watch TV, have a cup of tea or a glass of wine. Enjoy your baby, enjoy being with your partner and **CALM THE HELL DOWN!** I guarantee the world will not end because you strayed from the bedtime routine. Trust me, your baby will sleep (eventually). You have not failed. Your baby is consistently content and healthy and you've avoided losing your shit. I'd call that a success.

TOP TIP

If ever your baby does sleep, tell no one.

Do not speak of it, do not think about it, do NOT even acknowledge it.

If you do, your baby will find out and she will never ever sleep again.

PART III

HOW NOT TO LOSE FRIENDS AND IRRITATE PEOPLE

'90% OF BABIES SLEEP THROUGH THE NIGHT BY THE TIME THEY ARE SIX MONTHS OLD. 90% OF PARENTS ARE LIARS.'

THINGS I ACHIEVED IN THE FIRST NINE MONTHS OF MOTHERHOOD

1. I did not kill myself.
2. I did not kill my husband.
3. I had sex (the baby did not break my vagina!)
4. I did not punch anyone.

HOW NOT TO KILL YOUR PARTNER WHEN YOU HAVE BABIES

14

I had been married for about three years when I began to fantasise about killing my husband. In my defence, since becoming a father, he had become quite annoying (or possibly I had become more irritable). Either way, rarely a night went by when I didn't have the urge to stick a pillow over his fat, snoring face.

'The baby is awake,' I whispered loudly into James' ear on one particularly exhausting night. 'And it's your turn!'

'Can't you go, as you are awake anyway?' he groaned sleepily. 'I am so tired.'

'I swear one of these days I am going to kill you,' I told him.

'No you won't. You're too knackered,' he replied before swiftly going to check on the baby.

'I could poison you. That wouldn't take much effort,' I shouted after him. 'I've got some extra strong Toilet Duck under the sink. I could just pour it into your snoring mouth while you sleep.'

Some time later he returned to find me awake and Googling, 'Can Toilet Duck kill a human man'.

'Shouldn't you sleep while the baby sleeps?' James said, as he crawled into bed and went back to sleep, leaving me to my murderous fantasies.

I never did kill him. Partly because I was too tired and partly because his dead body would be tricky to move as he had put on a few pounds – selfish git. However, I certainly hated him for a while and I am pretty sure he wasn't too keen on me either. Things had changed so much since the baby was born that I became convinced our marriage was doomed. We barely spoke about anything other than our daughter or how tired we were. And as for romance? Well, that was well and truly dead. I believed that if I didn't do something we'd undoubtedly end up trapped in a loveless marriage for the sake of the children and he'd start shagging the milkman and I'd buy 16 cats. But fortunately I had a plan! A plan that would save our marriage! A plan that... I had read about once in a magazine in the doctor's waiting room.

'We need to go on a Date Night,' I announced one morning as I wiped crusty baby vomit from my shoulder. 'I don't want us to be one of those couples who stop making an effort. Do I smell like sick?'

So the deal was done. A few weeks later we persuaded my parents to watch the baby for the evening and headed out for a night of marriage-saving romance.

THE DATE NIGHT

'So we're finally out without the baby!' I said stifling a yawn, as we sat down in the trendy 'bistro' we had chosen for our big date. 'Look, there are candles on the tables with big burny flames and everything!'

'Woo-hoo! Let's get a drink!' James smiled enthusiastically as the waiter headed for our table.

'Oooh, let's have cocktails. Let our hair down and to hell with the consequences!' I said, rubbing my tired eyes.

'I'll drink to that!' James agreed and picked up a menu. 'Mojito? Sex on the Beach?'

'Wait!' I shouted. 'Thinking about it, the baby is bound to wake up later tonight. We'd better not get drunk.'

'Good point. How about a coffee?'

'Oooh, yes! I can't remember the last time I had a nice hot cup of coffee!' I grinned, hoping some caffeine might actually perk me up a bit.

'Wait! If we have coffee at this time it'll only keep us awake all night,' James pointed out.

We finally decided that it would be best all round if we just stuck with water. After all, we could enjoy a romantic meal out together without booze or caffeine.

'So what are you having to start with?' James asked, starting on the complimentary bread. 'I thought I would have the mussels and the slow-cooked pork.'

'I am starving! Oh, but have we got time for starters? We don't want to be home too late. We'll only regret it when the baby wakes us up at stupid o' clock in the morning.'

'Yes, you're right,' said James. 'What was I thinking? In fact, that pork might take a while to prepare. Maybe I'll just have a salad.'

'Good idea.' I nodded. Then I made the mistake of looking at the clock. I felt the panic rising as I saw it was 8.45pm. 'Oh my god, it's almost 9pm!'

'You know what?' James announced. 'We could just stick to this bread. Save time.'

'Yes, it is really good bread,' I said, hungrily reaching for a second roll.

So there we were, feasting on bread and water. Determined to be romantic and enjoy this time on our own together. But the exhaustion, in addition to the pressure of knowing that this was our one chance to enjoy a night out, left us struggling to find anything interesting to say.

'How was work?' I enquired desperately.

'Busy,' James replied. 'That new project means I had to create more spreadsheets and deal with the impact of the S09200 on the internal process system... Are you even listening?'

'Of course,' I yawned. 'I'm just really tired.'

'How was your day?'

'Not bad thanks,' I answered. 'Oh funny story. I lost my phone this morning. So I looked everywhere for it. Then I found it in my pocket. It was actually in my pocket the whole time!!' (Ok, so it was funnier in my head.)

'Ha, ha!' James (fake) laughed. 'How was the baby?'

'We are on a date. Let's not talk about the baby on a date. Tell me more about your spreadsheet thingy.'

'You want to talk about spread-sheets on a date?' He had a fair point.

So Date Night wasn't the romantic success we had envisaged. We ended up home and in our pyjamas by 9.30pm, taking it in turns to rock our baby to sleep. But as we laughed about our rubbish evening, I realised that things weren't so bad. Maybe they were just as they were supposed to be.

True Romance (Parent-Style)

When you have a baby it doesn't really matter about candlelit dinners or flowers. Romance is not dead. It is just taking a nap. You and your partner made a human together. A tiny person who you both have to keep in one piece and not totally fuck up. And you have to take care of her 24 hours a day without a break or barely any sleep. So it is totally normal to occasionally think about killing the love of your life with toilet cleaner (probably).

Fortunately, as James and I grew accustomed to the sleepless nights, things did get better. I gradually became less stabby and he learnt to be less annoying. We figured out that the secret to a happy relationship is quite simply empathy, tolerance and wine.

You may not have the time, energy or money for posh meals or weekends away. But if you sometimes change a nappy when it isn't your turn; if you never fail to take the bins out (I do the laundry, you do the bloody bins – that was the deal) then that, my friends, is true romance (parent-style).

So how do you avoid killing your partner when you have babies? Simply follow these post-baby relationship rules:

1: ALWAYS GO TO BED ON AN ARGUMENT

If the baby is asleep, then do not waste time doing anything other than sleeping. Chances are the argument was not that important anyway. Grievances like, 'You Flushed The Chain And Now The Baby Is Awake', 'I Wasn't In A Mood Until You Said I Was In a Mood And Now I Am In A Mood' and 'Who's Used The Last Of The Calpol And Put It Back In The Cupboard Empty' are just not worth the effort.

2: NEVER SAY WHAT YOU REALLY MEAN

In order to maintain marital harmony, there are some things that are better left unsaid, including any reference to 'being tired' (your partner will take this to mean you're suggesting you are more tired than them) and never admit to skiving off the baby.'

Instead, claim you are 'just popping out for milk', 'taking the bins out' or, my husband's favourite, 'I'm a bit constipated so I might be a while in the loo.' You both know that the other one is probably planning to sneak into the toilet with their smartphone for half an hour. But by not acknowledging that fact you save yourselves the effort of having to argue about it.

3: DON'T BOTHER MAKING AN EFFORT

Since we have had babies my husband and I spend a lot of time in our pyjamas, yawning at each other. Sweet nothings have become hushed whispers of, 'I am so knackered'. And 'Netflix and Chill' now means actual Netflix and chill. Your idea of a sexy text is no longer, 'I am not wearing any knickers,' but 'I am not wearing any knickers because you didn't take the laundry out of the bloody machine like I asked you to six times.' Forget flowers and hot dates. When you are sleep-deprived, simply going to the trouble of getting each other stuff is the height of romance. Nothing says 'I love you' more than fetching a forgotten toilet roll for your other half. There is little more alluring than being passed the remote control when you are too tired to move. And the words, 'Would you like a cup of tea?' uttered from your partner's lips are guaranteed to lead to the suggestion of

an 'early night' (wink, wink). Although nine times out of ten you will get into bed and realise you both want an actual early night – it really is the thought that counts.

4: DO NOT WORRY ABOUT SEX

When you have young babies it can be a challenge to find the time or energy to have sex. But try not to worry about it. The sex will still be available tomorrow, next month or even next year. You enjoyed sex before you had babies and one day you will enjoy it again.

5: CHILL THE HELL OUT

It is inevitable that some nights you will opt for sleep rather than sex and other nights you will opt for sex but get teething. You may choose to sit and drink wine in your pyjamas rather than go to a restaurant, or watch TV to avoid the effort of having to make conversation, but it won't be forever – so try not to worry. You are raising little humans together – falling in love with them more each day and watching in amazement as they smile, laugh or sit up for the first time. Becoming parents is exhausting, frustrating and challenging but it is also the most exciting thing you have ever done together. So empathise, sympathise, get stuff for each other, laugh together and you will survive.

15 A STEP-BY-STEP GUIDE TO SLEEP-DEPRIVED SEX

When you have babies, it can be a challenge to find the time for any active postnatal romance with your partner. After all, you are too busy dealing with postnatal everything else. But it is possible. Spice up your love life with this simple guide to sleep-deprived sex:

1. Decide to have an 'early' night.

2. Search the underwear drawer for something other than pyjamas. (Find baggy tee shirts, comfy 'period' knickers, two maternity bras, three used breast pads and/or a random thong that must have escaped the Great Thong Purge of 2010.) Opt for naked to save time.

3. Wonder whether you have time to give your underwear drawer a quick clear-out before all the sex.

4. Decide you better get on with it as the baby could wake up any minute.

5. Both jump into bed ready for action.

6. Realise you are both so tired you could do with an actual early night. Postpone sex until tomorrow.

7. Decide to have an earlier night.

8. Get into bed. Proceed to be romantic.

9. Partner thinks he hears the baby.

10. Both sit up and listen for the baby. Nothing.

11. Continue with romantic proceedings.

12. Think you hear the baby.

13. Both sit up and listen for the baby. Nothing.

14. Continue romancing for two minutes until the baby actually does wake up.

15. Get up and feed the baby. Return two hours later to find your partner is asleep.

16. Decide to have sex tonight no matter what.

17. That evening you are too tired for sex.

18. Two days later agree to definitely have sex that evening. Suggest doing it on the sofa to spice things up a bit (and to avoid falling asleep).

19. Begin romantic activity, but then spot Thomas the Tank Engine watching from under the coffee table. Turn Thomas to face the wall. Resume pre-sex activity.

20. Accidentally sit on Fireman Sam. Partner throws the Fireman Sam toy into the car box and restarts kissing.

21. Resist the urge to go and put Fireman Sam into the 'correct' toy box (because Sam is not a bloody toy car).

22. Continue thinking about Fireman Sam. 'That is clearly a box for cars. I have explained this system so many times. If we all put everything back in the wrong boxes we would never find anything.'

23. Accidentally bite partner's tongue due to angry kissing.

24. Partner asks whether you are still thinking about Fireman Sam.

25. Reassure partner that, 'I only have eyes for you my darling.' But take the opportunity to get up and move Sam.

26. Put Fireman Sam into the 'toy figures' box. While you are there, notice there is a stray block in with the cars. Put block away only to find a single piece of jigsaw in the 'block' box. Start searching through the jigsaw cupboard to find which jigsaw the piece belongs to. Until partner coughs.

27. Return to sofa for romance (dismissing all thoughts of jigsaw puzzle pieces).

28. Romance progresses to 'socks off' and partner leans in to whisper something into your ear... 'Can you smell piss?'

29. Both agree to put sofa sex on hold due to possible urine patch and watch TV instead.

30. Three days later the grandparents take the baby out for the afternoon, so you decide to spend the time having lots and lots of sex (followed by sorting out the toy boxes and underwear drawer).

31. As soon as grandparents depart, partner heads for the bedroom and takes off his clothes.

32. Explain that you can't just go from 'wiping a bum' to 'making love.' Suggest that 'having a romantic lunch and talking' would be nice first. Compromise by having tea and biscuits in bed.

33. Six minutes later both fall asleep.

34. Two weeks later decide you need a whole night away to have really good postnatal romance.

35. Leave baby with the grandparents and go to posh hotel.

36. Enjoy first night away together since you had the baby by eating, drinking, drinking some more and finally having fantastic, mind-blowing postnatal hotel sex (probably, you can't quite remember due to all the drinking).

37. Two months later, mind-blowing postnatal hotel sex is confirmed in the form of a positive pregnancy test. Now what could be more mind-blowing than that?

16

HOW TO PICK UP WOMEN WHEN YOU HAVE BABIES

Motherhood can be lonely, but if you are sleep-deprived it is a Catch 22. You crave adult company, but at the same time you are too bloody tired for adult company. Some days talking to anyone over the age of two seems like way too much effort. But on other days, you would quite like a moan, a laugh and a chat (ideally over wine) with someone who gets it. But it is hard to make friends when you are always tired. The exhaustion makes it difficult to hold a conversation; it impairs your mental filter, tramples over your inhibitions and makes it hard to concentrate on what is being said. So unfortunately, the sleep-deprived parents among us are not much of a catch.

A LOVE STORY: SLEEPLESS IN SAINSBURY'S

I loved my husband but sometimes I longed for something more, something new, something different...

'I need some Mumance,' I thought to myself as I headed for the local playgroup one sunny afternoon (while making a mental note to self not to say Mumance out loud to any of the mums). As I was new, I was keen to make a good impression in the hope that it would lead to me meeting someone special.

It was during a game of, 'Who is your weird crush?' that I seized my opportunity to impress the others with my 'wit'.

'Mr Tumble!' 'Chris Evans!' 'Cbeebies Andy!' The other mothers laughed. 'My dad!' I suggested, jokingly. Clearly, it was a JOKE, but they looked at me like I was some kind of freaky, dad-shagging pervert.

Things went from bad to worse as I tried to explain, 'I was kidding. I do not fancy my dad. I mean that would be weird. He's like old... and my dad, obviously. I know what you're thinking! 'She doth protest too much!' Anyone want a coffee?'

I never went back to that playgroup. Since that fateful day, I dabbled on the 'play-dating' scene. There was the One Who Drank Decaf and The One Whose Baby Learnt To Self Soothe In The Womb, not to mention The One Who Went To The Gym (For Fun). But I never met anyone quite right.

Until... The One. From the moment I saw her and her biscuit-covered baby in the supermarket, I knew I had to have her. I immediately recognised the familiar, 'What the hell am I doing?' expression on her face as she pushed her pram aimlessly down the baby aisle. Our blood-shot eyes met across teething gel.

'I have no idea what I have come in here for,' she slurred sleepily. I explained that I had forgotten what I needed too! 'I am pretty sure it's not these, though,' I laughed, pointing to a packet of flavoured condoms.

'Or these,' she replied, gesturing at some glow-in-the-dark ones. We laughed. We talked. She told me she had felt like a Zombie Shit Brain since having babies and I was smitten. So we exchanged numbers and went our separate ways.

The next day I texted her nervously, keen to arrange a date.

'Hi Zombie Shit Brain, it's Emily-Jane from Sainsbury's. Fancy going condom shopping again soon? HA!'

She never replied. I like to believe she simply forgot to text me back. But chances are she couldn't remember the condom thing and thought I was a weird sexter. Either way, it was clear that I needed to work on my pick-up technique before every mum in town thought I was a pervert.

Fortunately, as I got to grips with motherhood and embraced my sleep-deprivation, I eventually bagged myself some like-minded parent friends who would totally find that 'dad crush' joke funny (probably). I achieved this by coming up with a few unique ways to pick up tired women.

If you are sleep-deprived and in search of a friend, here are a few pointers:

1. AIM LOW

Let's face it. Those well-rested parents with clean hair and matching socks are well out of your league. They will discuss Annabel Karmel recipes, politics and the latest big TV show you still haven't got around to watching while drinking decaf lattes. You will end up looking like an idiot and it'll all end in tears. Your tears.

So aim lower. Look for the parents wearing dark glasses and stained clothes, who reek of dry shampoo and stale vomit. The ones surreptitiously using a baby wipe to clean a vomit stain from their leggings. These are the ones for you.

2. STALKING YOUR PREY

Finding yourself a sleep-deprived parent can be tricky on account of the fact that they are often too tired to leave the house. But there are a few places you might be able to pull one.

OLD PEOPLE CAFÉS: You may assume that Starbucks is the exhausted mums' hangout of choice, but the truth is many of them try to avoid those places. Instead they opt for the less popular back-street tea rooms, or simply grab a free coffee from Waitrose and drink it in the car. The thing is, tired mums are in cafés for the coffee only. We do not want to queue, bump into 'someone we know' or be asked questions. 'Flat white? Latte? One or two shots? Decaf? Medium or large? Drink in or takeaway? Something to eat with that?' Shut the hell up and give me caffeine!

CAR PARKS: Any sleep-deprived parent will know that you do not wake a (finally) sleeping baby. So when your baby falls asleep in the car, it is a rare opportunity to sit and do nothing until they wake up.

WALKING ROUND (AND ROUND AND ROUND AND ROUND) THE PARK: A sleep-hating baby will occasionally sleep in the pram, but only on the condition that the pram is moving. So although walking is an effort for the sleep-deprived parent, it is preferable to being Inside With A Grumpy Tired Baby.

3. MAKING YOUR MOVE

When wooing an exhausted parent, it is important to remember that less is more. If you rush straight in with conversation, you'll scare them off. Start with a smile that says, 'I, too, have no idea what I needed from this shop.' For maximum effect, follow up the smile by flicking your freshly dry-shampooed hair in their direction and yawning in their face.

4. SEALING THE DEAL

So you have met The One. You talked, you laughed, you moaned about how tired you are and you exchanged numbers… You feel like you have finally found someone who you can talk to. Really talk to. You know… about important stuff like, 'How to buy booze when you have babies with you, without looking like a massive wino' or whether Mr Bloom is really a gardener. Someone who won't get offended if you forget to reply to a text message or cancel plans at the last minute because you are too knackered to leave the house. Someone with whom you can drink coffee on your urine-stained sofa and put the world to rights (or maybe just talk about the weird crush you have on your dad. Joke!) A perfectly imperfect friend who *YOU MAY NEVER SEE AGAIN*. Because sleep-deprived mums are bad at making plans. They are forgetful, disorganised and rarely remember to return phone calls. But all is not lost. Thanks to the Internet, you can enjoy an effort-free friendship without leaving the house. Find each other on Facebook, Twitter or Instagram. Send each other selfies of you and your baby awake at 4am, swear about dinner time and moan about bedtime – *ALL FROM THE COMFORT OF YOUR FRONT ROOM!* Bide your time and then, one day, when you both start to feel marginally less knackered, maybe, just maybe, you'll manage to meet up in real life.

17

HOW NOT TO PUNCH PEOPLE WHEN YOU HAVE A BABY WHO DOES NOT SLEEP

Why is it that when you have a baby who does not sleep everyone else you meet seems to have a baby who does sleep? Don't get me wrong. I think it is great. I am honestly happy for these people.

I don't even mind when they tell me about it. Which they do. Every, single time I see them and that's totally fine. Sometimes they are even kind enough to give me unsolicited advice on how to get my baby to sleep. But as grateful as I am for their tips (usually delivered with a sympathetic head-tilt), it occasionally makes me want to punch them in their smug, fresh faces. And the worst thing about these well-rested parents is that they are so bloody nice. Therefore, not only do I want to punch them in the face, but also I want to punch myself in the face for having such horrible thoughts about lovely Mrs Smuggy McSmugface who has just asked, 'So, how is your baby sleeping now?'

I am not proud of myself. I never thought I'd be the kind of person who mentally assaults perfectly pleasant people. But it just reinforces the ridiculous myth that infants who sleep a lot are 'good' babies, while those of a more wakeful disposition are 'bad' babies or 'hard work'. And that is just not right. So I propose a revolution! Let's make bad sleepers the new 'good' babies.

Next time a fellow parent informs you that, 'Little Jack has been self-soothing since he was three weeks old,' or suggests that, 'You really should sleep train your baby,' simply smile and share with them the joy of living with a Sleep Thief.

Here are a few examples:

FELLOW PARENT: She is such a good baby! She goes to sleep as soon as I put her down in her cot!

ME: My little one is such a good baby. She likes to sleep on me so I get a lot of cuddles. There is nothing nicer than feeling your baby's heart beat in time with your own.

FELLOW PARENT: We are so lucky with our baby boy! We can take him anywhere and he just sleeps in his pram the whole time!

ME: We are lucky too. We can take our baby anywhere and she'll stay awake the whole time gaining valuable stimulation and interaction. She is so alert and entertaining.

FELLOW PARENT: We are blessed with our baby! She not only sleeps all night, but naps during the day!

ME: Our little one rarely sleeps during the day and wakes regularly during the night, so we get all that extra time with her. We are so blessed.

FELLOW PARENT: We can't complain! Our baby sleeps all day!

ME: My baby doesn't sleep during the day at all. But I didn't go through nine months of pregnancy and childbirth just to look at a bundle in a Moses basket. So, I can't complain.

FELLOW PARENT: Oh, your baby is still not sleeping? You look so tired. You poor thing!

ME: She is still not sleeping, but that isn't why I'm tired. It's all the activities we do together. We have baby sensory games in the morning, followed by crafts and stories, then I cook an Annabel Karmel meal from scratch for lunch. In the afternoon we have singing, stimulating outdoor play and swimming lessons. Finally, I whip up an organic casserole for dinner, and then it's on to a full body baby massage, more stories, bath and bedtime. This parenting game is rather exhausting, isn't it? You look amazing, by the way. Not tired at all.

FELLOW PARENT: Oh dear! Is she still not sleeping? Maybe she is teething or hungry?

ME: She is teething and hungry. In fact, that's the problem. She's so hungry she keeps eating her teeth. She is so bright.

FELLOW PARENT: My baby is so clever! She self-soothes herself to sleep.

ME: My baby is so clever. She has such an active mind that once she is

awake she finds it hard to get back to sleep. She's too busy doing mental arithmetic or something.

FELLOW PARENT: My baby is so considerate! She goes to bed really early, giving me plenty of time to go to the gym and burn off that baby weight.

ME: My baby is so considerate. She is helping me burn off the baby weight by allowing me to carry her around the house for 24 hours a day. In fact, I think I am fitter now than I was pre-pregnancy.

FELLOW PARENT: Oh, you let her sleep in your bed? You are making a rod for your own back there. She'll never sleep on her own.

ME: Never, really? Never? In that case I had better get a bigger bed. It is going to be a bit of a squeeze when she gets to eighteen.

FELLOW PARENT: Do you put her down drowsy but awake?

ME: (I am afraid a mental punch to the face is the only suitable response to that question.)

FELLOW PARENT: Have you tried putting her in her cot, turning out the light, shutting the door and leaving her to cry?

ME: Err... no, because I quite like my baby.

ENOUGH.

No more counting the days until our little ones Sleep Through The Night. No more crying into our coffee because we have been up since... last week. Instead, let's put on our best pyjamas and cherish every last tiring, wonderful, draining, glorious, frustrating, challenging, waking hour we spend with our exhausting little angels.

All babies are 'good' babies. Eye bags are the new black. Pyjamas are the new skinny jeans. Sleep-deprived is the new stylish. Spread the word and let's start the revolution today (just as soon as I've had a nap).

TOP TIP

How to Deal with Unsolicited Sleep Advice

1. Nod.
2. Smile.
3. Do whatever the hell you were going to do anyway.

PART IV

NO SLEEP SOLUTIONS –

A PRACTICAL GUIDE TO SURVIVING WITHOUT SLEEP

'99% OF NEW MOTHERS ARE TIRED BECAUSE AT NIGHT THEY BECOME FUCKING SUPERHEROES.'

THINGS I ACHIEVED IN THE FIRST EIGHTEEN MONTHS OF MOTHERHOOD

1. I did not die of sleep-deprivation.
2. I lost my shit at a carrot.
3. I hit the wall 234 times.
4. I drank 3 million litres of coffee.
5. I had another baby who would not sleep.

'SIRI, CAN YOU DIE OF SLEEP-DEPRIVATION? I HOPE SO BECAUSE THEY SAY YOU SLEEP WHEN YOU ARE DEAD...'

18

HOW TO SURVIVE WHEN YOU HIT THE WALL

hit the wall
1. When an athlete experiences a sudden loss of energy in a long race.

It often happens at night. When your baby wakes for the zillionth time and you just can't get out of bed. It sometimes happens at Dinner Time. You have been taking care of the children all day on barely any sleep and you are on your last legs. Last legs that you now have to stand up on and prepare something marginally healthy for your grumpy, tired child.

Sleep-deprivation has taken its toll on you both physically and mentally. You have lost your appetite and lost weight. You might even be experiencing dizzy spells, headaches or panic attacks. You are exhausted, tearful and have an overwhelming feeling that you cannot do this any more. You have hit the wall.

You want to run away: out of the house and away from the baby who relentlessly keeps you awake every night. You want to flee from your bedroom: the place that is no longer a sanctuary of rest and comfort, but a battleground of stress and tears. You long to go somewhere quiet and lie down on a massive bed: to a hideaway where you can sleep all night. Somewhere you can be on your own and not be nagged, poked, prodded or climbed on.

Some days you hit the wall so hard you just want to die because at least then **YOU WOULD FINALLY GET SOME BLOODY SLEEP!**

'This too shall pass,' you tell yourself. And usually these soothing words help, but sometimes they don't. Some nights you are so relentlessly exhausted that you long for silence and pray for sleep. You want to be alone. You want to cry. Because you are pretty sure motherhood has broken you. But it hasn't.

So next time you are up against the wall, try to remember that even after the darkest night the sun always rises in the morning. One smile from your baby will give you a reason to survive whatever life throws at you. It will give you the strength to carry on even when you feel like you can't. You may not feel strong right now, but you are. Strength is not making it to the morning playgroup or finishing the laundry. Strength is carrying on when you feel like crap but the only choice you have left is to get up and get on with it. Strength is not about being the best; it's about surviving when you are *not* at your best. So next time you hit the wall, take a deep breath and remember that you coped yesterday and the day before and the day before that. **THE WALL WILL NEVER WIN.** The Wall is a massive dickhead. Don't just hit it, punch right through it and you will come out the other side.

19 HOW TO GET THINGS DONE WHEN YOUR BABY WON'T LEAVE YOU THE HELL ALONE FOR FIVE MINUTES

Do you ever get to the end of the day and you know you have been busy, but you can't figure out what the hell you've been doing all day? You are exhausted, you can't remember when you last sat down and you have not eaten. But you look around the house, the washing up bowl is full of dirty dishes, the kitchen sideboard is littered with dirty socks, every available surface is covered with toys – and you are still in your pyjamas! So you ask yourself, 'What have I actually been doing all day?'

Before I had children I had it all worked out. I would look after the baby while my husband worked full time. It seemed like the ideal set-up. I could do some work from home, keep the house tidy, cook dinner, bake cakes and maybe even write a novel. And I would do all of this in the afternoons, while the baby napped. You see, pre-parenthood I assumed that all babies took naps. Long naps, all afternoon, and parents could use this time to catch up on sleep, have a cup of tea or get things done. I assumed wrong. My baby did not want to nap in the afternoon, or in the morning – or if she ever did it would only be on me! So my life became a constant battle to get things done so I could get some sleep, or get the baby to sleep so I could get things done.

But one day I had a brilliant idea that would solve all my problems. I would write a big Things To Do List and get my life more organised.
Here is my first (and only) Things To Do List:

THINGS TO (DEFINITELY) DO

1. Do ALL the laundry. Ensure washing basket is empty and all clean washing is put away and not just left in the baskets/on the floor/on the bed.

2. Clean the sofa to remove the vomit/stale milk/wee stains. (First buy sofa cleaning equipment) and perhaps just avoid inviting guests over who like sitting down.

3. Mend the broken remote control so the batteries don't fall out and the baby doesn't try to eat them.

4. Move the dirty baby sock from the kitchen sideboard * – it has been there a month. **DO *NOT STRAY FROM THIS MISSION*.**

* Now you may think that this is too simple a task to go on a To Do List, but this particular sock was the bane of my life. Every time I went to put the sock into the wash, something always prevented me from achieving my goal. I got close once. I actually picked up the sock. I headed towards the laundry basket with the sock. 'Look at me,' I thought. 'Not only am I looking after a baby on two hours' sleep, but I am moving the sock. Getting stuff done. Go me!' But then out of the corner of my eye I spotted the baby trying to eat a battery! I threw the offending sock back on the sideboard, ran to the baby and all sock-moving plans were immediately forgotten. **

** Since writing this book, the sock has finally been moved. I told James about my sideboard sock plight one night (yes, post-baby conversations are that riveting) and he simply picked up the sock and put it in the washing machine like some kind of sock-moving superhero. (By the way, he is not a big sexist who believes sock moving is a woman's job. He had either a) not even noticed the sock b) had noticed the sock but assumed it was where the socks lived or c) didn't care about the sock.)

5. Do a paediatric first aid course in case the baby chokes on a battery.

6. Start making delicious healthy home-cooked meals – this does not mean opening the fridge with every intention of making a healthy home-cooked dinner, and then opting for the easy option.*

* Since becoming a mum I have succumbed to the power of smiley faces. Whenever I open the freezer they are there. Beaming up at me. I would like to wipe the smile off their stupid, delicious faces. 'Eat me,' they cry. 'We are only potatoes. What is so bad about potatoes? Cook us with some frozen veg and fish fingers and you have a nutritious meal fit for a baby.' The grinning little gits had me at potatoes.

7. Stop buying smiley faces.

8. Take the baby to playgroup to ensure she will not turn out to be a socially inept weirdo who cannot sort shapes and is unable to perform all the moves to 'Wheels on the Bus'. ***

*** In my defence, my local playgroup takes place at stupidly early o'clock in the morning. I made it once and spent the entire session basically comparing my baby to the Veteran Playgroup Infants: 'Why is my baby not sorting shapes yet?' I panicked. 'That other baby just got the triangle in the correct hole twice. Mine is just licking the red square.'

9. Do more shape-sorting with the baby.

10. Get all the baby pictures developed.

11. Bake a cake (you are a mother now and this is what they do).

12. Buy a cake tin and a baking book.

13. Take all of the old baby clothes to a charity shop.

14. Finally watch *Breaking Bad*.

15. Clean the skirting boards.

16. Get my hair cut.

What was I thinking back then? The sleep-deprivation had clearly made me delusional. My children are now three and five years old and I have only completed two of these tasks! I mended the remote control and got a haircut (well, trimmed my fringe with the kitchen scissors). So how do you get things done when your baby won't leave you the hell alone for five minutes? You don't… but that is ok. Use your tiny reserve of energy wisely and don't waste it scrubbing skirting boards or baking cakes.

Think about it. What is the very worst that will happen if you don't wash the dishes today? Will somebody die? Will you fall ill? Will you be arrested or even punched in the face? No. I'll tell you the very worst thing that might happen. You might need a drink and have to wash up a cup.

Sometimes we get so caught up in getting things done that we forget how to just *be*. We get so worried about all the things we *should* do, we neglect to do the things we *want* to do. So today, sod the stuff on the To Do List and follow this list instead:

THINGS TO DO TODAY

1. Survive.

ALTERNATIVE SLEEP ADVICE FOR SLEEP-DEPRIVED PARENTS

Thanks to the Internet, parenting 'experts' and celebrity nannies, new parents have baby advice available to them 24 hours a day. Unfortunately, most of it is totally useless to the tired parents of a totally normal human baby. But help is at hand because The Institute Of Real Life People With Actual Babies has come up with some alternative advice for you and your baby:

THE 'EXPERTS' SAY – Sleep when the baby sleeps.
THE INSTITUTE SAYS – The very fact that you are reading this advice is because your baby *doesn't* sleep. So on the rare occasion she does nap, the best thing you can do is drink coffee.

THE 'EXPERTS' SAY – Put your baby down drowsy but awake.
THE INSTITUTE SAYS – Put Your Baby Down Practically Comatose Or Not At All Or They Will Make You Pay.

THE 'EXPERTS' SAY – Give your baby a 'dream feed' before you go to bed.
THE INSTITUTE SAYS – Never wake a sleeping baby. Don't touch or even breathe near your Sleep Thief or she will wake up immediately.

THE 'EXPERTS' SAY – Place an item of your clothing in the cot with the baby.
THE INSTITUTE SAYS – Get in the cot with the baby. This is the only way anyone is going to get some sleep.

THE 'EXPERTS' SAY – Wean them off the night feeds.
THE INSTITUTE SAYS – Don't wean them off the night feeds. If they work for you then stick with them for as long as you can, as they are an easy and convenient sleep inducer.

THE 'EXPERTS' SAY – Look out for your baby's sleep cues and then put her in her cot.
THE INSTITUTE SAYS – Look out for the baby's sleep cues and then quickly grab your smartphone and the remote and stay where you are until the baby falls asleep. You may be baby-trapped, but at least you are sitting down and it is quiet.

THE 'EXPERTS' SAY – Establish a consistent bedtime routine.

THE INSTITUTE SAYS – The key to a successful night awake is to avoid getting stuck in a consistent bedtime routine. Babies change their wants and needs all the time. What is working now may not work in two weeks' time.

THE 'EXPERTS' SAY – Teach your baby to settle itself to sleep.

THE INSTITUTE SAYS – Teach yourself to settle down and chill the hell out. Stop worrying about teaching your baby to sleep because one day she just will...

FUN FACT

100% OF HUMAN BABIES SLEEP THROUGH THE NIGHT EVENTUALLY

21 HOUSEHOLD HACKS FOR TIRED PARENTS

I used to have a clean house, clean clothes and clean hair. Then I had children and before I knew it I was spraying my hair with Febreeze and drowning in a sea of dirty laundry. However, thanks to the following energy-saving tricks, I now have a marginally passable abode:

1. Get bigger cupboards. Mess isn't really the problem. It's the fact that you can see it. Invest in some big solid cupboards and simply shove anything causing a mess inside them. Then lock the door and walk away. When it comes to creating a beautiful family home, it's what's on the outside that counts.

2. Wear a blindfold. Alternatively, keep your eyes covered at all times.

3. Place all the items you no longer need in bags to take to the charity shop. Leave the bags in the bottom of the big cupboard until you DIE. Then they will be someone else's problem.

4. Send the children to stay with the grandparents for a night. Take a bulldozer to your house.

5. Move into a brand new home. Leave your family to live in their own muck.

6. Never tidy up until ten minutes before guests are due to arrive. You will somehow achieve more in that ten minutes than you have done all week.

7. Better still, never have guests and live happily in your own filth. Problem solved.

8. Get the kids to help. Babies and toddlers love eating crap off the floor. Instead of vacuuming, invite some friends with kids over for a play date and let them tuck in.

9. Avoid those hard-to-reach places. If you can't reach them, you probably can't see them. Live in ignorant bliss and never ever look under the sofa.

10. Get drunk. After a few drinks, even those annoying sticky handprints on the television can look kind of cute. 'It is not mess! It was my kids making memories... or something. Now pass the wine.'

11. Divide dirty laundry into three piles: darks, lights and delicates. Set fire to them.

12. Don't ever clean the house. Leave it to get so bad that your family call up a reality TV show and they send someone round to clean it up for you.

RECIPE: HEALTHY, HOME-COOKED FAMILY MEAL

Buy fresh ingredients.

Take fresh ingredients out of the fridge.

Stare at ingredients blankly.

Pour a glass of wine.

Put a pizza in the oven.

One week later, remember about the healthy home-cooked family meal.

Take out the fresh ingredients.

Realise they are all out of date.

Pour a glass of wine.

Put a pizza in the oven.

22

HOW TO LOSE YOUR BABY WEIGHT WITHOUT EVEN TRYING

Dear New Mum Who Thinks She Looks Like Crap,

If you have just had a baby, I am not going to lie to you – you probably do look like crap. You have dark shadows under your eyes, your hair is a mess and you probably aren't going to fit back into your skinny jeans any time soon.

But right now? Who the hell cares? You made a human being with your body. That is amazing. You have a new lifestyle, a new child and six million new things to worry about. A few extra pounds does not need to be one of them. **YOU HAD A WHOLE PERSON IN YOUR STOMACH, FOR GOODNESS SAKE!** A person you now have to take care of 24 hours a day on barely any sleep. Trust me, you are going to need all of that cake.

I know what you're thinking. It's not as simple as just deciding not to care. You say that you feel ugly and fat. You look in the mirror and you see a roll of fat where your stomach used to be and stretch marks and cellulite on your once smooth skin. You notice the wrinkles across your forehead, the age spots creeping over your cheeks and the tiny creases in the corners of your eyes.

But let me tell you what I see. I don't notice the dark circles around your eyes. I see the love in your eyes when you look at your baby. I don't see your frown marks. I see a fearless expression on your face that comes from knowing that without a shadow of a doubt you would do anything to keep your child safe. I don't see the extra pounds. I am too busy watching the wonder in your smile when you watch your baby do something for the first time. I see a Mother. I see beauty.

Still not convinced? Then look at your baby. See how she gazes adoringly into your eyes? She is not thinking, 'Put that biscuit down you fat cow!' She is thinking, 'I love this womb container who actually made me. She is amazing. She keeps me alive by feeding me from her own body!'

Look at your partner. See how he watches you feed your baby? He is not thinking, 'Wow, she really needs to get down the gym or I am never having sex with her again.' He is thinking, 'She grew our baby inside her body. She is more beautiful than ever.'

You might look different since you had the children, but 'different' does not mean worse. Your body has evolved into something more wonderful and more powerful than ever.

So stick your unwashed hair up in a Mum Bun and wear those baggy pyjamas with pride. You will sleep again. You won't always look like crap. And one day – thanks to the Taking Care Of Babies Diet – you will even get back into your skinny jeans. But for now, don't sweat it. Save your worrying for the bigger stuff. Because trust me, now that you are a mum there will be bigger stuff. But please remember, just because you feel like crap does not mean you are not beautiful. Motherhood is the new black. Stop worrying and go eat cake. You deserve it.

Love from a Mum Who Doesn't Give A Crap About Looking Crap

THE ONLY POST-BABY DIET PLAN YOU WILL EVER NEED

When I had just given birth the last thing on my mind was, 'How will I ever squeeze into my jeans again?' It was more, 'Will I ever have time to get dressed again?'

If I managed to get into any clothes – vomit stained or otherwise – that in itself was an achievement. And even on the days I did get dressed, it was normally a toss-up between snot-covered leggings or jeans that smelt of urine. I would be more likely to wonder, 'Do these leggings smell?' than, 'Does my bum look big in this?' In fact, I would describe my post-baby style as, 'If It's Not Poo, It'll Do'. But I can confirm that thanks to my Post-Baby Diet Plan I did eventually lose the baby weight.

HERE IS MY SIMPLE, EFFORT-FREE GUIDE:

1. GIVE BIRTH TO A BABY

A human being and a big bag of afterbirth have just left your body. That is most of the weight shifted right there.

2. FORGET THE GYM

Once you have had your baby, any excess fat will soon drop off because you will never sit down again. Not standing up will become such a rare luxury that from now on you will consider getting stuck in a traffic jam a 'treat'.

3. STAY UP ALL NIGHT – SLEEP IS FOR WIMPS

Remember those crazy days when you would go to bed at night and, you know, just go to sleep? Burning no calories whatsoever? Fortunately, those days are behind you. Welcome to the Nocturnal Parenting Gym.

Workouts include: getting up, picking up the baby, standing, swaying and walking around the house carrying a baby at least ten times a night.

4. CARRY STUFF AROUND – 24 HOURS A DAY

From the moment you give birth you will be carrying stuff and/or a baby around for about 24 hours a day. To achieve maximum results, invest in a heavy car seat, a complete travel system pram, a changing bag full of crap, a baby carrier and an infant who refuses to be put down.

5. THE POST-BABY DIET

Life with a newborn guarantees that most days you will not have time to eat. You will put toast in the toaster, pour cereal into a bowl or half make a sandwich, but you will never get around to consuming it. Even on the days you do have time, you'll be too tired to chew, let alone cook. Dinner also becomes a tricky business because babies hate their parents eating. They are perfectly happy in their bouncer until you pick up your fork. At that precise moment, your smiling bundle of joy will become a screaming monster that demands you put down your food and feed them instead.

TOP TIP

For a delicious, effort-free sandwich:
Take alternate bites of bread and
cheese. Lick butter to taste.

6. FEED YOUR BABY
Breastfeed to get the calories literally sucked out of you. Or formula feed to burn calories while making countless trips up and down the stairs to make up bottles of milk while holding a screaming baby.

7. CHILL THE HELL OUT
Unless you are sitting around all day eating lard and cakes, it is very likely that your body will eventually go back to its original shape and size. And as research shows that stress slows down the metabolism, then not giving a shit about your post-baby body is actually the best way to lose the baby weight.

HOW TO SURVIVE TWO UNDER TWO ON BARELY ANY SLEEP

'So, have you thought about contraception?' asked my GP at my six-week postnatal check.

'Contraception?' I scoffed and pointed at my new baby. 'Are you serious? I'm too tired to even think about sex!'

'But you might feel different in a few weeks' time?' she smiled, handing me a leaflet.

Weeks? I thought, throwing the leaflet in the bin. My vagina is going to be traumatised for way longer than that. Besides, I am not a bloody teenager. I know about safe sex. Patronising cow.

Nine months later...

'You know that time we kind of had some sex? The only time we had sex since the baby was born? Well, I'm pregnant,' I said to my husband. 'Surprise…'

'Oh yay! Shall I go and get us a bottle of sparkling wine to celebrate?' said James, trying his best not to hide the panic in his voice.

'Nah, I'm too tired,' I replied before crying into my ginger tea.

Don't get me wrong, we always planned to have another child but this was a little sooner than we envisaged. We figured we would wait until… you know… we'd had at least some bloody sleep first.

'At least the baby phase will be out of the way,' people assured me when I announced I was pregnant again.

But I didn't want it out of the way. I wanted a little rest first. How would I take care of two children without a bloody rest? So I spent most of my second pregnancy worrying about how on earth I would survive with two babies under two and, worse still, what if Baby Two didn't sleep either?

Well-meaning friends and family tried to reassure me. 'Don't worry; second babies are always good sleepers. You usually get one who sleeps and one who doesn't,' they said.

They lied.

Two Under Two in Six Easy Steps

If you are about to embark on two children under two, here are a few hot tips:

1. **Do not bother trying to get anything done, ever.** While it is tricky to get stuff done with one baby, with two of them it is practically impossible. I have lost entire days trying to get things done and achieved nothing. So I suggest you just do what you can when you can. Your To Do list should look like this:

> **THINGS TO DO**
> 1. GET UP.
> 2. TAKE CARE OF THE KIDS.

2. **Do not try to get anywhere on time.** Remember when nipping out for milk simply meant leaving the house and going to the shop? Once you have two little ones in tow, you will never 'pop out' anywhere ever again. From now on, it will take hours of tears, tantrums and nappy changes before you even get out of the front door. And then, inevitably, when you do get to the shop you will have forgotten what the hell you went in there for.

3. **Do not beat yourself up for occasionally losing your shit.** When you have two under two somebody always wants something from you. A banana, a biscuit, a drink, a dummy, a boob, a bottle, a nappy change, food, lunch, breakfast, a snack, toys, clothes, a story, a carry... Your life becomes an endless cycle of getting stuff for small people. Some days you'll want to quit. Other days you'll totally lose your shit because you have had no time to think, breathe or have a cup of coffee. But you still get them the stuff.

Because at the end of the day, you would do anything for these two tiny terrors (plus it is far easier than being nagged for stuff for what feels like the rest of your life).

4) LOVE CONQUERS ALL. When you are expecting your second baby you will secretly worry whether you will love him or her as much as you love your firstborn. Surely it must be impossible to love another human being as much as you love your eldest? There could never be a baby as cute, as funny, or as beautiful. Then Baby Two arrives and he or she is just as cute, just as funny and just as beautiful. And before you know it, you can't imagine life without them both.

5) GET AN EXTRA PAIR OF EYES TO PUT IN THE BACK OF YOUR HEAD BECAUSE, AT SOME POINT, YOUR CHILDREN WILL TRY TO KILL EACH OTHER. Not intentionally, of course. But toddlers have no sense of the difference between 'funny' and dangerous. Here are some examples: 'It would be so funny to whack my baby sister over the head with a mug' and 'I wonder what will happen if I stick this pencil right up my sister's nose.'

6) BUY TWO OF EVERYTHING. Siblings always want what the other one has. The toddler could pick up a dead frog and the baby would still drop whatever she is doing and decide she desperately wants that dead frog more than anything in the world. You can tell them to share until you are blue in the face. But apparently 'share' is toddler speak for 'snatch'. I would also suggest that all the children's cups and bowls are the same colour – trust me on this one.

Having two children close in age can be exhausting and frustrating. Rarely will there be a day when you have not silently sworn about something. But it is also pretty amazing. For every stressful moment there is a special moment and although there are days when you will lose your shit, there are also days when your heart will melt with love. And it is always a great comfort to know that no matter what, your children will always have each other.

So fortunately (with the help of even more coffee, wine and other survival techniques), I did survive two-under-two. And these days (when they are not trying to kill each other), my daughters are best friends. I can honestly say that having two children close in age was the best thing I have ever (accidentally) done.

A GUIDE TO LEAVING THE HOUSE, BUYING MILK AND OTHER COMPLICATED TASKS

'I should do something today,' I said to myself after a very long and tiring night with the baby. 'I can't just stay home all day in my pyjamas again. I should try to do something useful.'

I necked a coffee and felt marginally more awake. 'Right, I am going to the supermarket.'

But the trouble with coffee is that it can trick you into thinking you are not a severely sleep-deprived mum at all, but some kind of supermarket-visiting superhero. One mug of the strong stuff and you suddenly believe you are capable of great feats... like going out for milk with two kids under two. However, once the caffeine wears off, chances are you'll find yourself wandering aimlessly around the shop and crying over the unexpected items in your bagging area... The truth is that it is one thing looking after babies while you are sleep-deprived in the safety of your own home where there is children's TV and you don't have to communicate with adults. But outside? Outside there are grown-ups and conversations and traffic lights. Outside is a whole lot harder.

So that morning's coffee must have been a particularly strong brew because not only did it fool me into thinking that I could go grocery shopping with a baby and a toddler in tow, but also, I could do it without a list.

'I only need four things! What kind of idiot needs a list for four things?' I laughed, like I was some kind of grocery-getting genius.

'Even I can remember toilet roll, nappies, washing-up liquid and milk!' I declared and off we went to the shop... without a list. 'You can do this' whispered the caffeine as I made my way outside.

Unsurprisingly, by the time I made it to the supermarket I'd totally forgotten everything I needed to buy. I racked my brain to recall my shopping list while attempting to stop the toddler hitting the baby with a bottle of tomato sauce.

It was only once I was halfway back to the car that it all came flooding back to me: toilet roll, washing-up liquid, nappies and milk!

Although I was too tired to face going back into the shop, I knew if I returned home empty-handed I would feel like a failure. So there was only one thing for it. The only thing you can do when faced with a decision while sleep-deprived. Drink more coffee.

I decided that my best option was to give the kids enough biscuits so I could drink a free coffee in Waitrose, and then get back to the job in hand. But it is never that easy…

'Toilet roll, nappies, washing-up liquid and milk. Toilet roll, nappies, washing-up liquid and milk,' I muttered to myself as I necked my coffee and embarked on my shopping.

'I want a carrot,' yelled the toddler, grabbing a carrot from the shelf. 'You don't even like carrots,' I told her, putting the carrot back.

'I want a carrot,' she shouted and retrieved the carrot.

I could sense the good people of Waitrose looking at me. 'What kind of mother doesn't let her child have a carrot? She let her have three biscuits in the café!'

'Okay, you can have the carrot,' I sighed, as the exhaustion tried my patience. 'We can have carrots for dinner, how about that?'

'I don't want carrots for dinner. I don't like carrots,' she screamed, loudly. I screamed quietly and the baby started crying.

I took a deep breath and spoke to the toddler through gritted teeth. 'If you want the carrot darling, you can have the carrot. If you don't want the carrot, then *PUT. IT. BACK.*'

The toddler then threw the carrot on the floor and I am ashamed to say I lost it. 'For god's sake. Do you want the stupid bloody carrot or not?'

'Carrots aren't stupid,' she cried.

At this point, both my offspring were crying and I felt like the worst mum in the world. I just wanted to go home but then this trip would have all been for nothing – and because of a stupid carrot. I would not let that crunchy little dickhead win.

We finally got home in one piece with toilet roll, nappies, washing-up liquid and a carrot, but **NO MILK**. Damn it.

The worst thing about sleep-deprivation is that it makes everything so much harder. A shopping trip, a doctor's appointment or posting a letter all become major operations. You struggle to get your head around simple tasks and feel totally overwhelmed if you try to do too many things in one day.

So take it from me, if you have been up all night with a baby, do not listen to super strong coffee. It lies. Stay home and do as little as possible. Ignore the voices that tell you that you should go to playgroup, take the kids swimming, go to the park, clean the house, do some laundry, wash the dishes... because you do not need to do any of these things.

If you had been up all night before you had children, what would you have done the following day? I am guessing nothing? And you wouldn't have felt the slightest bit guilty about it. Because back then you knew that when you felt run down and deprived of sleep you needed time to recharge your batteries. So why is it different now that you are a parent? Do you think anyone else gives a damn if you spend a day in your pyjamas watching telly? Other mothers are too busy with their own shit to worry about what you are doing. Your friends and family definitely do not give a damn. Your baby certainly doesn't care. So why do you?

The truth is when you have babies even when you are doing nothing, you are doing something. You are taking care of your family. You are making sure they are fed and clean and safe and happy. You are tending to their needs every minute of every night and every day despite being exhausted. Keeping a human being alive is not nothing. So give yourself a break!

SURVIVAL STRATEGIES FOR SLEEP-DEPRIVED PARENTS

After reading all of the 'hot' tips for tired parents on the entire Internet, I was still feeling like shit. So I came up with my own survival guide:

1. Just so you know, you are probably going to get fat, have heart disease and suffer from anxiety and depression… There, now you don't have to waste time Googling the adverse effects of sleep-deprivation. You're welcome.

2. View sleep as a luxury, not a necessity. This way, any amount of sleep you get is automatically a bonus!

3. Do not go out in public if you have been up all night. There are people out there and you may have to talk to them.

4. Try to remember you are not a 'bad' parent. Being sleep-deprived can sometimes make your parenting less than perfect, but don't beat yourself up. You are not a bad mum for feeding the children fish fingers for three nights in a row. It will not scar your children for life to watch television for

two hours straight. And you will not burn in hell if you bribe them with biscuits!

5. Sleep-deprivation won't kill you. Despite how bad you feel, you are not actually going to drop dead from lack of sleep. At worst, there is a small chance you might almost pass out. Some days you might feel like you can't go on, but you will survive.

6. Treat yourself. I am not sure why drowning your sorrows gets such bad press. I am not encouraging alcoholism – but I find if you reward yourself with a little treat once the kids are asleep it makes getting through the bedtime battle more bearable. And for me a treat is a glass of wine!

7. Never ever look at the clock in the middle of the night. You will only panic about how little sleep you have had.

8. Do not attempt to do anything until you have had a large cup of coffee. It may have to be reheated several times, but it will be worth it.

9. Forget multi-tasking. Do not try to do more than one thing at a time. This will only result in jobs being left half done so you will end up 'multi-half tasking'. I currently have three half-written articles, four pending email replies, one polished shoe and I have been doing the same load of washing for three weeks.

10. Maintain a healthy diet. By 'healthy,' I mean food. By 'diet,' I mean remember to eat.

11. RECIPE: SLOW-COOKED STUFF

Ingredients: Chopped up savoury edible stuff and stock

Method:
• Put everything in the slow cooker and turn it on.
• Open the slow cooker at dinnertime and you have a delicious(ish) home-cooked meal (that does not contain fish fingers).
• Enjoy feeling like a brilliant mother (for about five minutes until the kids demand fish fingers).

12. Instead of beating yourself up about all the things you should have done, commend yourself for all the brilliant things you have done. Such as washing your hair, not breaking any crockery and keeping a baby alive all day long.

13. Do not buy any books about how to get your baby to sleep. Unless they are specifically written about your baby, they are useless.

14. If you find yourself with an Extreme Waker Who Laughs In The Face Of Sleep, you are probably at the point where if anyone else suggests anything you really should or should not be doing you are very likely to head butt them. Avoid violence at all costs. It uses too much energy. Simply nod, smile and walk away. At this stage, the only thing you should be doing is to get yourself and your baby to sleep by Whatever Means Necessary.

15. Take mini power naps on the go. When you have a baby who will not nap, there is no chance whatsoever of 'sleeping when the baby sleeps'. So instead you need to sneak in a bit of shuteye wherever you can. Seek out traffic jams and long supermarket queues or, if you are pushing the pram on a straight path, take the opportunity to close your eyes for a while.

16. Acceptance. There is only one thing worse than being sleep-deprived and that is getting stressed about being sleep-deprived. 'How will I look after the kids on no sleep? How can I be a perfect parent when I am so tired? If I don't sleep surely I am going to DIE?' Well, guess what? You do not need to be a perfect parent; you just need to be a parent. Once I accepted that my baby would probably not sleep much for the foreseeable future, but we would be okay, I started to feel a whole lot better.

17. See the funny side. Come on, you are so tired you just put a shitty nappy in the fridge and the milk in the bin. That is pretty hilarious! Remember how you got your own daughter's date of birth wrong for the first two years of her life (true story)? Or when you said, 'love you' to the postman instead of 'thank you'? Pure comedy. Learn to laugh, otherwise you'll only cry… and possibly never stop.

18. Find fellow Sleep Thief Victims and confide in them. Talking (i.e. moaning) to other sleep-deprived parents can really save your sanity. Misery loves company.

TOP TIP

Did you know that 99% of parenting problems can be solved with biscuits?

PART V

WHEN YOU CAN'T FIND THE LIGHT –

SLEEP-DEPRIVATION VS POSTNATAL ILLNESS

'99% OF NEW MOTHERS FORGET THAT THEY ARE ONLY HUMAN.'

THINGS I ACHIEVED IN THE FIRST TWO YEARS OF MOTHERHOOD

1. I did not break the babies.
2. I did NOT break.

25

THE THING THAT SLEEP COULD NOT FIX

I remember the exact moment I realised that I was a terrible mother. It was late afternoon and I was sitting in my pyjamas covered in vomit. I had thrown up while trying to force myself to eat something, and the baby had been sick all over me. This was not how I had pictured Motherhood.

I knew I would be tired, but I did not expect insomnia, anxiety and a complete loss of appetite. And it was all terribly inconvenient, as I had a brand new baby to take care of.

My family were convinced I simply needed a good night's sleep, friends thought I had the baby blues, but I knew the truth – I was rubbish at babies. When I left the hospital and brought my first baby home I wasn't filled with happiness. I was filled with sheer panic. I was struck with the overwhelming feeling that I was not going to be able to look after her. But what could I do? It was too late. I couldn't quit and go back to my old life. I wished I could put her back inside me, where I knew I could keep her safe. But I couldn't. So I cried. A lot.

Time passed in a blur of milk, nappies and tears. I could not think clearly and began having panic attacks. Then things went from bad to worse. I began to hallucinate. On several occasions I looked up at my husband and saw my baby's face where his should have been. Other times I imagined my daughter was actually part of my chest – like we had been welded into one being during the night. I saw faces in the darkness taunting me, watching me fail as a mother. It was terrifying. I felt out of control and I was petrified that I was going mad.

My husband was at a loss as to what to do. His paternity leave was up and he was also struggling with new parenthood and exhaustion.

'Is this normal?' I asked myself. 'I am a terrible mother and a weak person. Some people would give anything to have a healthy baby, yet I am acting like it is the end of the world.'

My anxiety got so bad that the thought of leaving the house filled me with fear. What if someone tried to hurt my baby? Snatched her from the pram? What if I couldn't stop them? What if I passed out and my baby was left alone? What if I lost my mind and left the pram somewhere? Any noise was magnified tenfold. The baby crying, people's voices, the cot mobile or any sound above a whisper would bring on a panic attack. I was constantly in a fuzzy-headed dreamlike state, as if I wasn't really there. I felt like an alien roaming a world in which I did not belong.

I got to the point where I didn't want anyone to see that I was this horrible, ungrateful mother. So I avoided people and didn't talk to anyone unless I had to. It felt as though I had disconnected from everyone and everything around me, including my baby and husband.

'Everyone hates me and I don't blame them,' I told myself. 'I have ruined this magical time for them all.'

 'Is this normal?' I asked the health visitor.

She told me there was a very good chance I was suffering from postnatal depression (PND) and advised me to go and see my doctor. But I did not believe I had PND. My perception of the illness was largely based on the news stories I had read about mothers harming themselves or their children, and TV dramas showing women with PND who felt no love for their offspring.

'Look, I haven't got postnatal depression,' I told her. 'Seriously, I am just rubbish at babies and really bloody tired. If I could just get some sleep, I'd be okay.'

'You have postnatal depression,' the doctor later explained.

She wanted to give me anti-depressants. I asked for sleeping pills, convinced that sleep would make everything ok. It didn't. So I went back to the GP. I was referred to a cognitive behaviour therapist and given medication. However, my clouded mind kept telling me I did not need to take the anti-depressants. I still believed that I was simply not cut out for motherhood and no number of pills could cure that. So I stopped taking them. Besides, if I was actually clinically depressed I wouldn't be able to get out of bed, right? The next day, I couldn't get out of bed. I wasn't eating and I had lost a lot of weight. I was still unable to sleep and I continued to have panic attacks. I was afraid to walk down the stairs with the baby in case I fell or lost control of my mind and dropped her. So in the end, I felt the best thing to do was stay in bed. I had everything I needed to look after a baby. Nappies and breasts. Sorted.

As I lay there listening to my baby cry for another feed, I remember thinking that my life was over. I honestly believed that this was how things would be forever.

That night my husband came home to find me and the baby in floods of tears. I told him I couldn't cope. He said he couldn't cope. We called my parents. It was decided that we would all go and stay with them and they would help take care of the baby – and me.

Back in my old bedroom, I felt like a young kid again. While I was comforted by the familiarity of my childhood home and grateful for the support of my family, I was so ashamed. I had a baby of my own now, yet here I was being looked after by my mother.

Despite all of this, I still refused to believe I was ill. As far as I was concerned I was simply a terrible mum and a weak, pathetic person who was not up to the job. I hated being a burden to everyone. I saw the way my family looked at me with what I imagined was disappointment, but was actually concern. I wanted them to think I was happy and confident. Enjoying taking care of my baby. So I came up with a brilliant idea. I would simply pretend to be okay. I would speak to no one about my dark feelings and worries.

From that day on I was determined to try to get back some physical strength. For the next few weeks, I ate small portions of plain food until gradually I found I could eat without throwing up. I was still barely sleeping. I had terrible insomnia and my daughter would wake up every hour. My nights were filled with silent tears and quiet despair. But as soon as I was physically capable of looking after my baby alone, I went home to put my plan into action.

To the outside world, I seemed fine. I got dressed, wore make-up and smiled, but inside I felt nothing but pain. My secret pain. I fed, changed and held my daughter, but I was doing it all under a black cloud. I didn't know who I was anymore. I truly believed I was getting it all wrong. That I was a failure. I loved her, but I felt no joy in being a mother – just guilt, fear and self-hatred. My child deserved better than me.

But the thing with suffering in silence, I discovered, was the longer you keep it a secret, the more it hurts. Eventually, tired and broken, I went to the cognitive behaviour therapist and admitted the truth about how I was feeling. She made me understand that I was very ill and she began to treat me for severe postnatal depression and anxiety.

As I continued with cognitive behaviour therapy (CBT) and started to attend a local postnatal illness support group run by the charity Home-Start, I finally understood that none of this was my fault and I wasn't a weak person. As my mind grew clearer, I realised that the fact I was able to take care of a baby – while also being ill and sleep-deprived – made me a strong person. And since my daughter was happy and healthy, I *was* a good mother. Slowly but surely the cloud began to lift and my symptoms improved. It was a long and difficult process of therapy and support, but it worked. I was determined to get better for my family and I did. Which was just as well really, because I had a second baby on the way...

Fortunately, by the time I became a mother-of-two I was still sleep-deprived and I still found motherhood challenging – but I was no longer drowning. I had hope. I knew that no matter how tired I was, I could cope. I would survive.

26

ARE YOU DEPRESSED OR JUST REALLY BLOODY TIRED?

Are you feeling anxious, tearful and overwhelmed since becoming a parent? Probably. You have just given birth to a little human being and now you somehow have to not break her on barely any sleep.

'But isn't motherhood meant to be wonderful? I have a cute baby with tiny little fingers and toes.'

Didn't I mention that you've had stitches in your lady's bits, piles and you haven't slept. Plus, there's the raging hormones to deal with.

'Yes, but look at her little baby grow! It says 'I love mummy!' This should make me happy. Now I am crying again. I am crying all the time. Shouldn't I be happy?'

No. This gig is tough. Newborns are hard work. Just because you do not feel happy 24 hours a day doesn't mean you are *not* happy to have a beautiful baby. It means you are human.

Tearfulness, anxiety, loss of appetite or increased appetite, lack of motivation and irritability are all symptoms of both sleep-deprivation and depression. Then there's the fact that exhaustion can make you feel low, but depression can make you feel exhausted. Hence the reason why so many cases of PND go undiagnosed. The mother often believes she is just totally and utterly shattered.

I was that mother. Before I was diagnosed with postnatal depression (PND), I spent a long time convinced I was just really bloody tired. People kept telling me I would be okay after a good night's sleep. But even after I had managed to get some rest, I still felt exhausted, anxious and depressed. When I had my second baby, I was sleep-deprived but I did not have PND. While I still felt exhausted, anxious and depressed, it wasn't as all-consuming and I could see beyond it. I didn't feel so hopeless. So although many of the symptoms of PND and sleep-deprivation were very similar – how my healthy mind and my unwell mind responded to those symptoms was very different.

Every case of PND is different, but this is how it went for me:

PND VS SLEEP-DEPRIVATION

PND: I can't sleep. Even when the baby is actually asleep.

SLEEP-DEPRIVATION: The baby is asleep so I can sleep.

PND: I still feel tired even when I have slept.

SLEEP-DEPRIVATION: I feel so much better after a good night's sleep.

PND: My child is not sleeping because I am a crap mother.

SLEEP-DEPRIVATION: My child isn't sleeping because she is a baby.

PND: I am struggling with motherhood because I am a weak person.

SLEEP-DEPRIVATION: I am struggling with motherhood because I am really bloody knackered. But I'm only human.

PND: I can't cope any more.

SLEEP-DEPRIVATION: I can't cope until I have had coffee. Then I will cope. Just like I did yesterday and the day before that.

PND: I hate myself.

SLEEP-DEPRIVATION: I hate being sleep-deprived.

PND: Everything is shit and it will be forever.

SLEEP-DEPRIVATION: Sleep-deprivation is shit, but it will pass.

PND: I am a failure.

SLEEP-DEPRIVATION: I am exhausted.

GIVING DEPRESSION THE FINGER

Postnatal depression is manipulative. It floods your mind with self-doubt and negative thoughts. It convinces you that you're hopeless, a bad parent and a weak person. And the more you believe it, the stronger it gets. Depression is determined. It wants to stay. It will trick you into believing you cannot do the things that will ultimately make you better, such as talking, finding support, leaving the house, taking medication or going to therapy.

DEPRESSION IS BASICALLY A DICK

If you are a parent dealing with depression or anxiety, then reading the following list will really piss it off! So read it now quickly – before depression makes you feel bad for reading it instead of making baby food out of organic unicorn tears.

1. You are not a weak person. You are suffering from an illness that happens to be depression. You got sick; it is not your fault.

2. You can still be a good parent when you feel anxious, sad or just plain terrible.

3. Postnatal depression is more common than many people think, affecting around one in ten women. You are not alone.

4. Postnatal illness can come in many different forms. Just because you are up – and wearing make-up – does not mean you don't need help as much as the mum who can't get out of bed. Pain is pain, whether it is under the skin or on the surface.

5. Your baby will not remember seeing you cry. Your baby will be fine.

6. You are taking care of your child while feeling awful. That is something to be proud of.

7. If your baby is happy, healthy and all in one piece then you are doing a great job.

8. You will try to convince yourself that you are not ill. That you are just a bad parent. This is not true. It is the depression talking. Tell it to shut the fuck up.

9. At some point you may worry that you have gone mad. But you haven't.

10. Postnatal illness does not discriminate; it can happen to anyone – working mums, stay-at-home mums, dads and even film stars like Gwyneth Paltrow!

11. You have nothing to be ashamed of. Depression is a disease. You did not choose it.

12. You have nothing to feel guilty about. Would you feel guilty about having a physical illness?

13. Talking will help. There is significant evidence to show that sufferers of PND improve more quickly with support. Find a support group, get counselling, ask your GP about cognitive therapy or talk to family and friends.

14. If you are taking medication, it does not mean you are weak. A diabetic would not think twice about taking insulin. Anti-depressants do not change who you are – but they can help you to find your way back to who you were before you got ill.

15. It is okay to take a break. You need to look after yourself. After all, you can't drink from an empty cup.

16. Even people who aren't suffering from a mental illness find parenthood really tough. You are stronger than you think.

17. Just because you are not cherishing every moment right now does not mean you don't cherish your child.

18. Those things you are worrying about that might happen? The 'what ifs'? It is more than likely that they will never happen. Depression plants these seeds of doubt in your mind. Do not nurture them and they will not grow.

19. You may not feel strong, but you are. Strength is carrying on when the only choice you have is to wait it out. Strength is not about being the best; it is about surviving when you are at your worst.

20. You will get better and when you do you will be stronger than ever. In fact, you may even win at sleep-deprivation!

PART VI

HOW TO WIN AT SLEEP-DEPRIVATION

'YOU DON'T LOSE YOURSELF WHEN YOU BECOME
A PARENT; YOU FIND A STRONGER, WISER
(AND MORE TIRED) VERSION OF YOURSELF.'
– ME

**THINGS I ACHIEVED
BECAUSE OF MOTHERHOOD**

1. I wrote a book!

2. I made two awesome children.

SLEEP TRAINING FOR GROWN-UPS

Good news for tired mums and dads! The Institute Of Real Life People With Actual Babies has launched a new sleep-training method designed for parents.

This simple technique was developed after a recent study revealed that adult humans are much better at learning than baby humans. Research has proved that since a newborn baby has spent most of her life inside a female without access to parenting manuals or Google, she does not know a lot of stuff. In 100 per cent of cases, infants were found to take a significant amount of time to get to grips with simple tasks such as Holding A Thing or Rolling Over and often up to three or four years to learn Not To Poo Their Pants.

Research proved that grown-ups, on the other hand, could be trained to do all manner of complicated tasks including driving motorcars, deep sea diving and even molecular physics. The study concluded that, based on this evidence, teaching the average adult NOT to sleep through the night for a short period of their life should be relatively simple.

STAYING AWAKE SUCCESSFULLY IN SIX EASY STEPS

This simple method, known as the *F.U.C.K.I.T* approach, has been proven to make parents less stressed, more confident and only slightly addicted to coffee.

F   Forget about the 'expert' advice.

U   Use your instincts and common sense.

C   Coffee.

K   Keep smiling. Laughter is the best medicine.

I   It will pass. Remember that.

T   Take care of yourself so that you can take care of your baby.

HOW TO CHANGE THE WORLD (OR NOT) ON BARELY ANY SLEEP

I remember the night I decided to change the world. I had spent two years taking care of two sleep-hating babies and it had finally dawned on me that I would probably not die of sleep-deprivation. So I announced to my husband, 'I will write a book! A book that will normalise infant night wakings and revolutionise the way society views babies' sleep. I will save tired parents from the likes of SuperSmugNanny and rescue discontented babies from Gina Ford! I will help mums and dads to laugh in the face of exhaustion.'

'Do you know that J.K. Rowling actually wrote Harry Potter in a café while her baby slept next to her in a pram? Well, I have a baby and a pram. Tomorrow, I am going to Costa to change the world!'

'If you are going to town can you pick up some loo roll?' asked James. Idiot.

The next day I got my 'Carpe diem!' on. I packed the toddler off to my mum for a few hours, strapped the baby in the pram, bought myself a posh new notebook and headed to the café to write my Great World-Changing Book. Except things didn't quite go to plan. This is what I wrote:

MY BOOK
(WRITTEN IN A CAFÉ JUST LIKE ROWLING)

This is not a brilliant start. I have nappies, rice cakes and wipes, but I do not have a bloody pen.

I asked the Costa boy if he had a pen I could borrow, but he only looked at me as if I was mad. I strongly suspect he thinks a pen is a kind of Italian biscuit. I explained I needed **TO WRITE SOMETHING DOWN** (I even mimed writing) but he just shook his head apologetically. Does no one use actual pens any more?

Shit. I have spilt coffee on my new notebook.

A lady at the next table has taken pity on me and given me a grubby pen (definitely stolen from the bank) from the bottom of her bag. She said I could keep it. I told her I would dedicate my first novel to her. In hindsight, this might have been a bit of an extreme way to thank someone for the loan of a dirty pen.

The baby is asleep – hooray – so here goes!

Ok, I am finding it really hard to start my Great Book as the pen woman is staring at me. Does she think I lied about needing to write something down, just to get a free pen? Costa boy is also watching me, I suspect to see what one does with a 'pen', but it is all very off-putting. I bet Rowling didn't have this problem. I bet she had a pencil case full of pens. Brilliant, now I can't concentrate as I am starting to panic. It is a race against time before the baby wakes up. I'll just carry on writing crap while pulling my best 'deep in thought about something really important' face, for a bit. This café is bloody noisy. I bet Rowling didn't write Harry Potter in a noisy café. It was probably a lovely quiet little tearoom full of little old ladies and spare pens.

Pen woman is still staring at me. Maybe she is waiting for me to ask her name for the book dedication.

BABY IS AWAKE. DAMN IT.

Fobbed her off with a biscuit. It seems she does not want to sleep in the pram like Rowling Junior so Plan B is in operation. I feed her stuff to keep her quiet while I start my book. (Is this how obese Britain started?) Baby is looking at me covered in biscuit and saliva. She does not look happy. She threw the remaining biscuit on the floor so I gave her a rice cake. She threw that on the floor, so I gave her the rest of my Costa lemon drizzle cake. She seems happy with that. She should be at £2.99 a slice! Right, here the hell I go... Or not. Baby has finished the cake and is doing her poo face. DAMN IT.

Baby is now covered in cake, screaming and smelling like poo.

I better go change her. Might as well get the frigging loo roll so it is not a completely wasted trip.

The **BLOODY** end.

As I headed home with a coffee-stained note book, dirty pen and some
toilet roll, I concluded that JK Rowling must have had one of those magical
angel babies who fall into a long, deep sleep anywhere, any time, giving
their mothers a chance to change the world in peace. I felt like a failure.
I was convinced that I would never achieve anything because my babies
would never sleep and I would be tired forever.

I just wish I had known back then that one day, in the not-too distant
future, I would achieve something *because* my babies did not sleep. And
despite having battled with postnatal depression, hitting financial rock
bottom and enduring four years of severe sleep-deprivation, it would be
okay in the end! I wish I had believed there would be light at the end of the
tunnel, it would pass and it was all temporary. I finally learnt that when life
throws you lemons you have just got to look life in the eye and say, 'You
know what? I fucking love lemons, so the joke is on you.'

30 THE CURSE OF THE MUMMY (SOMNIA)

I remember the first time it happened. I had wanted it for so long that it almost didn't seem real. In fact, the next morning I wondered whether it hadn't just been a wonderful dream.

THE BABY SLEPT THROUGH THE NIGHT!

For eight hours straight, I did not have to get out of bed and feed, change or cuddle a small child. I did not have to make a drink, find a dummy, sing, shush, walk, rock or explain to anyone that it was time to sleep.

You would assume that the next day I woke up so refreshed I washed my hair, did six loads of washing, put the clothes away in the actual wardrobe, made spaceships out of cereal boxes, left the house with two young children in tow in five seconds flat, went to the shop for milk (and actually remembered to get the milk), didn't swear or burst into tears at all and cooked a delicious family dinner from scratch. That I finally got to be the perfect mum I always planned to be before I actually had babies. However, none of this would be true. Because apparently, when you have been sleep-deprived for so long, you lose the ability to sleep through the night. Mumsomnia is a thing, people, and it is rubbish.

My daughter was about 15 months old when it happened. I had just crawled into bed after a long day, desperate to snatch some sleep before she unleashed her nightly Oh-Are-You-Going-To-Bed-Mummy?-Then-Let-The-Games-Begin scream.

Ten minutes passed and I remember wishing she would just get it over with and put me out of my misery. However, an hour later she had still not woken up.

I allowed myself a small glimmer of hope, 'Could tonight be the night that she… sleeps through? **OH MY GOD, THE THINGS I COULD DO TOMORROW IF SHE SLEEPS THROUGH!** Maybe I'll drive to the park farm, do a big shop, meet friends for coffee, I could even hoover under the settee. I should write a Things To Do list… right now. Just in case. Or maybe I should just sleep.'

Midnight came and went and I was still awake. The baby was still asleep. It had been four hours! Four whole hours. When four hours became five hours and I was still not asleep, I started to get a bit worried. 'What if the baby is not asleep, but in some kind of coma?' I thought in a panic.

I nudged James, 'James! Wake up! It's the baby.'

'Not my turn,' he groaned sleepily.

'No,' I explained. 'She is asleep.'

'You woke me up to tell me the baby is asleep?'

'No. You don't understand, she has been ASLEEP ALL NIGHT.'

'What?' he yelled, as shocked as I was, before leaping out of bed and heading for the baby's room.

Five minutes later he returned. 'She is fine. Just sleeping.'

'I know that! But why?' I asked.

'Well, she is probably tired. Like me,' he said, getting back into bed.

'Goodnight.'

As I desperately tried to get some sleep, I started to imagine what life would be like if I was no longer tired. What if there were no more night-wakings, no more children sleeping in our bed, no more twilight lullabies? What if I never again got to lie down with a young child on my chest listening to her breathing as she drifted into dreamland? What if I was never needed ever again for midnight cuddles and reassurance? After having two babies who did not sleep, I could barely remember how it felt not to get up during the night. My entire life as a mother had revolved around trying to get babies to sleep, trying to get some sleep myself and attempting to look after babies and myself on barely any sleep.

So, what now? I thought to myself. For many years I had blamed not being a perfect parent on sleep-deprivation. What if I was unable to step up to the mark when I was no longer exhausted? Would I be on time for everything? Go to all the playgroups and make home-cooked meals every night? Would I start doing arts and crafts? Would I have matching socks again? Would I go out with friends at night? Go back to work full time? Write my book?

But then it hit me. What if I couldn't do these things? What if I was simply the kind of parent who is better at fairy stories than fairy cakes? What if I was rubbish at making papier mâché castles? What if I still lost my shit at dinnertime or continued to hide in the loo for a little cry on a bad day?

Some time after 5am, sleep finally engulfed me like a warm hug from an old friend... until 6.30am when I was rudely awoken by my family.

My daughter didn't sleep through the next night or the night after that... In fact, it wasn't until she was about two and a half that she did it again. But although I had not quite reached the light at the end of the tunnel of tiredness, I was starting to see the occasional small ray of sunlight...

31

THE AMAZING BENEFITS OF BEING A SLEEP-DEPRIVED PARENT

We are always being told about the negative aspects of having a baby who doesn't sleep, but what about the good stuff? According to the Internet, the sleep-deprived among us are well on our way to becoming obese, diabetic and depressed. But did you know that there are actually some pretty amazing benefits to being woken up night after night after night?

In fact, I almost feel sorry for parents of the Magical Sleeping Angel Babies because after four years, two dream-crashing kids and around 6.2 million night wakings – I am positively reaping the rewards of all those sleepless nights.

HERE ARE JUST A FEW OF THE PERKS:

1. YOU HAVE A REALLY BLOODY CUTE GENIUS BABY

A recent study by The Institute of Real Life People With Actual Babies revealed that infants who wake up a lot during the night are Really Bloody Cute. Research shows that Sleep Thieves are designed extra adorable as a way of preventing their parents from selling them on the Internet. There is also a theory that gifted babies need less sleep. My daughter can fit an entire fish finger in her mouth while singing 'Let It Go'. Gifted! Clearly.

2. YOU GET A LOT OF 'ME TIME'

Sleep-deprived parents spend many hours lying in a dark room next to, under or feeding a baby. So why not put this time to good use? Since becoming a mother, I have mentally written a sitcom, two novels, this book, single-handedly solved the refugee crisis, almost devised a plan to take over the world and, well, pissed around a lot on Facebook.

3. YOU GET MILLIONS OF CUDDLES

I don't know about you, but one of the main reasons I had a baby was to have something really cute to cuddle. So I am living the dream because my babies love to cuddle me – 24 hours a day! Why sleep at night when you can have hugs, kisses, tiny toes poking you in the face and cute little fingers gouging at your eye balls? #blessed

And that is not all! Cuddling has health benefits too! It releases the 'love' hormone oxytocin, which reduces stress, boosts the immune system, relieves anxiety and makes you feel happy.

4. YOU ARE THE ENVY OF ALL YOUR PARENT FRIENDS (VERY OCCASIONALLY)

When the Well-Rested Parents are falling apart after poor teething Wilfie woke up twice in one night – this is your chance to shine. As they cry into their decaf tea, take the opportunity to give them a Not-So-Smug-Now head-tilt before swooping in with a strong coffee and a hug (see No. 3, above). Once you start regaling them with tales of your baby's twice a bloody hour wakings, they will soon feel much better about their life. You'll become the saviour of the very slightly sleep-deprived!

5. YOU LOSE THE BABY WEIGHT WITHOUT EVEN TRYING (OR CARING)

The great thing about having a sleep-hating baby is that you get a lot of free exercise! Taking care of a Sleep Thief day and night burns a hell of a lot of calories. Not that you have many calories to burn. Because chances are you don't get time to eat. I once survived a whole day on a banana and three pickled onions. I may have been weak and undernourished, BUT I WAS BACK IN MY SKINNY JEANS, BABY! Well, I could have been... If I hadn't been too tired to get dressed.

6. YOU ARE MORE IRRITABLE AND ANGRY

Lack of sleep makes you more prone to losing your shit, but this is not a bad thing! It is well documented that it is unhealthy to 'keep things bottled up'. Well, thanks to sleep-deprivation, I uncork my bottle of anger on a regular basis and I am so much happier for it. It is great! Like the time when I was peeling potatoes and the toddler started screaming for potatoes. I explained I was making her potatoes right now, but she screamed even louder so I swore and threw the bloody potatoes out of the window, one by one. But it was all good because I wasn't bottling that rage up. I was throwing my rage right out of the window with those Maris Pipers. Go me!

7. YOU LOSE YOUR MEMORY

An impaired memory is one of the most useful benefits to being a sleep-deprived parent. You have a great excuse for forgetting things. Simply follow up your apology for being late, forgetting a birthday, a name or an appointment with, 'I am so sorry, my baby has kept me up all night!' And all will be forgiven. Nobody is going to hold it against a poor tired mother and, even if they do, who cares? You won't remember anyway.

8. YOU HAVE A VALID EXCUSE NOT TO LEAVE THE HOUSE

Home is the best place to be when you are tired. There are comfy chairs and you don't have to wear clothes or talk to people. Once you have cancelled enough nights out/parties/play dates due to sleep-deprivation, the invites will eventually stop coming altogether – giving you extra time to spend with your bundle of joy.

9. CRAP IS THE NEW BLACK

Good old sleep-deprivation ensures that you are totally comfortable with letting yourself go. Gone are the days when I made the effort to look pretty. Since being sleep-deprived, I consider myself 'dressed up' if I am wearing matching socks and clothes without snot on them.

10. YOU ARE THE TRUEST VERSION OF YOURSELF

Sleep-deprivation makes you lose your inhibitions. You are way too tired to care what people think of you or your parenting skills, which is actually a big plus! Okay, you may talk quite a lot of bollocks, but at least you are honest and what people see is what they get.

11. YOU GET TO DRINKS LOTS OF COFFEE

You may have liked coffee before you became sleep-deprived, but now you LOVE IT, DREAM OF IT AND LIVE FOR IT! Next to my family (and possibly wine), coffee is the best thing in my life. Not only does it give me a feeling of unadulterated euphoria, it convinces me I can do All The Stuff. That I am capable of anything! Seriously, I once did two loads of washing and cooked dinner in an actual pan after a particularly good cup. Coffee is to the sleep-deprived what spinach is to Popeye.

12. YOU BECOME A SUPERHERO

They say, 'Sleep is for the Weak'. They tell us, 'Sleep is for Wimps.' I have no idea who 'they' are, but they are on to something. Sleep-deprivation is a form of torture and yet parents are not only surviving it – they are taking care of children at the same time! Some nights they might cry tears of frustration. Some days they might hide in the toilet praying for the strength to make it through dinnertime. Yet, every day they get up and get on with it. Sleep-deprivation may try to break us, but in fact it makes us stronger!

13. YOU FEEL LIKE YOU'RE DRUNK (WITHOUT WASTING MONEY ON ALCOHOL)

Having a baby who wakes up throughout the night is basically like having free booze. Forgetfulness, talking rubbish, clumsiness and waking up feeling like crap are common symptoms of both sleep-deprivation and intoxication. We may be stuck with exhaustion for a while, but rest assured our livers and our wallets will reap the benefits. Shattered is the new smashed. Tiredness the new twatted!

14. Good things come from bad (sleep)

The best thing for me about having babies who did not sleep was writing about my babies who did not sleep and connecting with so many funny, strong and inspiring sleep-deprived parents from all over the world. After launching my blog and Facebook page, I finally discovered that sleep-thievery is rife and my children are normal! I was not bad at babies! So I wrote a book about it in the hope that it would make new parents feel less alone in the tunnel of tiredness. Then I became, really rich like J.K. Rowling and lived happily ever after. The end. (Come on, it could happen? But probably not).

So in conclusion, being a sleep-deprived parent is totally awesome. But I am afraid that there is some bad news I must share with you. Like all good things, it will come to an end. Sadly, research shows that 100 per cent of infants will definitely sleep at night time, eventually. So cherish these tiring times my friends, because all too soon the midnight hugs, snuggly pyjama days, the glory of that first sip of coffee in the morning, the feel of a sleeping baby on your chest – will be nothing but a distant memory. Unfortunately being a sleep-deprived parent is only temporary. So enjoy these wonderful benefits while you can.

32

HOW TO REALLY AND TRULY GET YOUR BABY TO GO TO SLEEP

Have you almost passed out doing Pantley or cried yourself out following Ford? Are you too damn tired to try another stupid sleep solution that probably won't work anyway? Then help is at hand! In my quest for sleep, I finally stumbled across a technique that worked for my babies.
The effort-free **G.O.T.O.S.L.E.E.P** method is designed for the extremely exhausted and guarantees to get any baby to go sleep... eventually.

G Get yourself ready for bed before you start your baby's bedtime routine. Babies can take several hours to fall asleep, so you need to be comfortable and ready to slip straight into your own bed with your baby once you have given up trying to put her down in her cot.

O Organisation is key to a successful bedtime. Before you begin baby's bedtime routine, empty your bladder and ensure your smartphone is fully charged. Trying to get your baby to sleep is a good opportunity to enjoy some quality screen time. You may be trapped under a baby, but you have the world at your fingertips.

T Transfer Ready. Is your baby drowsy but awake? Then she is not Transfer Ready. Wait until she is in a deep sleep. Then wait another ten minutes, just to be sure. Recent studies have revealed that 99 per cent of babies believe that drowsy but awake is bollocks, so do not make the transfer too soon.

O Only you. If your baby refuses to sleep anywhere other than on you, then rest assured this is completely normal. The solution is simple. Stock up on coffee until the phase passes.

S Sleep crutch. It is very useful to make a rod for your own back. If your baby will only sleep in bed with you, let her. (Although, this is not advisable if you smoke, drink alcohol or sleep on a bed of nails, etc.) If she will only settle after a feed, then feed her. If you need to rock or sing her into dreamland, do it. These failproof sleep-inducing techniques have been successfully getting infants to sleep since babies were invented.

L Learn *NOT* to sleep. In the beginning, trying to get a baby to sleep when you have been awake for three days is tough.

But do not fear. Eventually your body will become accustomed to the sleepless nights and you will get better at parenting while exhausted. Plus studies show that 100 per cent of sleep-deprived humans survive parenthood.

E Eye contact. It is very important that you make eye contact with your baby when settling her at night. That adoring look she gives you is often the only thing that will stop you from selling her to a travelling circus.

E Escape. The baby is finally asleep! Sleeping babies have the ability to sense when their parent is about to leave the room. To avoid waking the baby, you must exit with extreme caution. Do not breathe, do not rush and whatever happens do not look back.

P Pour yourself a large drink. Once you have left the baby's room, immediately pour yourself a glass of wine and relax (for about 15 minutes until the baby wakes up again).

33

THE LIGHT AT THE END OF MY TUNNEL OF TIREDNESS

My eldest daughter is the original Sleep Thief. The one that simultaneously broke me and made me. She stole my sleep but in return she gave me strength and stamina.

During the first few years of her life she barely slept so I barely slept. She hated her cot. She would not be put down drowsy but awake. She wanted to be held all the time. I thought it was all my fault. I thought I was a rubbish mother, a failure. I thought I must be doing something wrong. I had read the articles by the baby 'experts'. I knew the score. She would grow up all wrong. Her poor tired brain would be underdeveloped, her body obese, her social skills poor and she would lack independence and confidence.

She is five now. She can read, write and socialise as well as all the other kids in her class. She's happy, healthy, outgoing and bright. She was not broken. And the only thing I did wrong was to read the books and not my baby. The only thing I was rubbish at was not trusting my own instincts as a new mum.

But she turned out just fine. More than fine. She is funny, fearless and kind. She is beautiful inside and out. She inspires me every single day. She made me a mother. The mother I am today. And despite all the sleep crutches I apparently 'created for her,' despite the rods I made for my own back – she no longer sleeps like a baby (waking at night, wanting feeds, cuddles or just to dick about). She actually **SLEEPS**.

Although those first few years of motherhood were tough, in between the darkness and the sleep-deprivation there was beauty. Moments of joy that passed all too soon. But of course, I may have been too tired to see it at the time…

I only wish I could go back and enjoy all those moments that I missed because I was too busy worrying about 'making a rod for my own back' or reading books about how my baby should or should not be sleeping. I wish I could experience my babies as the mother I am now. The mother who knows she will not die of exhaustion. The mother who is all too aware that now those times are gone she yearns to have them all over again. The mother who trusts her maternal instincts and who realises that four years of night wakings is actually no time at all.

I remember… Feeding my new daughter in the dead of night. Exhausted and, I remember, overwhelmed. Crying for respite, praying for her to sleep so I could go to bed. My hot tears flowing into my breast milk.

I wish I could go back and enjoy the warmth of her at my breast one more time. Back to the time she needed me so entirely. Back to when I, alone, was her nourishment, her comfort and her world.

I remember... Lying beneath my sleeping daughter, wishing she would sleep in her cot rather than on me. Putting her down, picking her up, putting her down, picking her up. Engulfed by feelings of frustration.

I wish I could go back and feel her sleeping on my chest one last time. I wish I could stroke her head, listen to her soft breathing and feel her heart beating in time with my own.

I remember... My baby singing and laughing in my bed at 4am. Totally unaware that the world was asleep. I felt stressed and tired, so tired.

I wish I could go back and laugh with her in the darkness. Enjoy one more all-night pyjama party with my daughter.

I recall... Breastfeeding my one-year-old. She would suckle until she fell asleep. It felt like forever. I longed for her to hurry up, so I could go.

I wish I could go back and have that moment once again. I always assumed there'd be one more feed. I can't even remember the last time. The truth is, I was probably on my mobile as she fed. Texting my husband, 'when will this end?' or scrolling social media. I was there, but not there.

During the day my daughter would never nap. I would spend hours trying to get her to sleep so I could do 'stuff'. The house would be a mess. There was so much washing. Then she would grab my leg, wanting to play, wanting a cuddle. I needed to tidy up. I needed to do 'stuff'. 'In a minute,' I would say. 'In a minute.'

I wish I could go back for one more day and leave all those chores. Enjoy more cuddles, read another story, play another game, forget the nap.

My daughter would never go to bed. It was always one more story, one more lullaby, one more drink. One more cuddle. 'Will you lie down with me, Mummy?' She would ask. 'When will she fall asleep on her own?' I would fret. 'When will bedtime not take hours?' I would get impatient for some time alone, to gather my thoughts, to spend time with my partner. So I rushed the songs. I rushed the cuddles.

I wish I could go back for one night and lie down with her for longer. To enjoy cuddling her to sleep and making her feel safe.

Not so long ago I had just climbed into bed. It had been a stressful week and I was tired. My eldest rarely needed me during the night any more. But that evening she called out to me: 'Will you lie down with me, Mummy?' I snuggled up next to her and sang her a lullaby. She fell asleep with her hand in mine and I whispered in her ear.

'Goodnight, my little Sleep Thief. Thank you for all the long nights, relentless wakings and the endless cuddles. Thank you for giving me so many moments to cherish.'

THE END

ACKNOWLEDGEMENTS

I always wanted to write a book. Unfortunately, before I had children I was far too busy and tired. What with the entire evenings to myself watching TV, and weekends spent down the pub or nursing hangovers and binge-watching box sets…;) Then I had babies and was *actually* busy and tired for the first time in my life, yet… I managed to write a book. But I could not have done it without the help and support of a few brilliant people!

Thank you to my parents for supporting me and inspiring me to follow my dreams and a special thanks to my mum for being my first editor and making sure I don't swear too much. Thank you to my determined agent Jane Turnbull, who believed in my book right from the start and tirelessly fought to find it a home, the team at Kyle Books for expertly turning my manuscript into a book and talented illustrator Lorna Cowley for bringing my words to life!

I would never have even got close to writing a book had a few people not helped me survive the dark times, including the charity Home-Start Leicestershire and my cognitive behavioural therapist, Laura from Let's Talk Well-being.

A HUGE thank you to all of my lovely, hilarious followers on social media and private Facebook support group members for making me laugh and making me feel normal during my journey through sleep-deprivation.

I must thank my husband, James, for inadvertently providing some material for this book and for always believing in me. I will be eternally grateful to my daughters Isla and Cleo for relentlessly keeping me awake and inspiring me to write this book in the first place. They not only made me a mother and a better person, but they have made all my dreams come true.

But, biggest thank you of all goes to Coffee. I could not have done this without you.